… E. Ambrose

'An … ar II

'The n… rld War
that I have …
Joseph Heller

'History boldly told and elegantly written . . . Gripping'
Wall Street Journal

'Ambrose proves once again he is a masterful historian . . .
spellbinding'
People

D-Day

'*D-Day* is mostly about people, but goes even further in evoking the horror, the endurance, the daring and indeed, the human failings at Omaha Beach . . . Outstanding'
The New York Times Book Review

'Definitive . . . His evidence is overwhelming'
Wall Street Journal

'Packed with drama and information, never losing sight of the horrors of combat, Ambrose's *D-Day* is the best book yet on what many historians consider to be the most important day of the 20th century'
San Francisco Chronicle

Wild Blue

'Mr Ambrose's storytelling ability is unparalleled'
Wall Street Journal

'A brilliant new book'
USA Today

'Ambrose is a superb historian'
The New York Times Book Review

Other books by Stephen E. Ambrose

Band of Brothers
D-Day
Citizen Soldiers
The Victors
Nothing Like It In The World
Comrades
The Wild Blue

For Hugh,
with whom I've watched so many
John Wayne movies,
here is another adventure story—
except that this time it is all true

PEGASUS BRIDGE

D-DAY: THE DARING BRITISH AIRBORNE RAID

STEPHEN E. AMBROSE

SIMON & SCHUSTER

London · New York · Sydney · Toronto · New Delhi

A CBS COMPANY

First published in Great Britain by Simon & Schuster UK Ltd, 2003
This edition published by Simon & Schuster UK Ltd, 2016
A CBS COMPANY

1 3 5 7 9 10 8 6 4 2

Simon & Schuster UK Ltd
1st Floor
222 Gray's Inn Road
London WC1X 8HB

www.simonandschuster.co.uk

Simon & Schuster Australia, Sydney
Simon & Schuster India, New Delhi

A CIP catalogue record for this book is available from the British Library

Paperback ISBN: 978-1-4711-6318-0

Printed and bound by CPI Group (UK) Ltd, Croydon, CR0 4YY

FSC
www.fsc.org
MIX
Paper from responsible sources
FSC® C020471

CONTENTS

PREFACE

In 1984, on the 40th anniversary of D-Day, the British had to make a difficult choice—where to concentrate their celebration. The Americans had chosen their beaches, Omaha and Utah, and the British were tempted to do the same. They could have gone to Lion Sur Mer, near the center of Sword Beach, or to Arromanches, on Gold Beach. Arromanches would have been especially appropriate, because it was there that the British placed the artificial harbors, built at tremendous cost by British industry and representing a triumph of British imagination, technology, and productivity.

Instead, the British centered their celebration on the tiny village of Ranville, some ten kilometers inland from the coast. Ranville had been the D-Day headquarters of the British 6th Airborne Division. Prince Charles came there and participated in a moving memorial service in the military cemetery. There were hundreds of airborne veterans present, and thousands of spectators, plus photographers, reporters, and television crews.

The veterans paraded past Prince Charles, who is the Colonel-in-Chief of the Parachute Regiment. As the bands played, the old men marched past with glistening eyes, proudly wearing their berets, their chests covered with their medals. Norman men and women lined the streets, four and five deep, waving, cheering, weeping.

Prince Charles had flown to Ranville; on the way, he passed over and studied intently a small, nondescript bridge over the Caen Canal, two kilometers from Ranville. It was a bridge that had been captured by a gliderborne company of the 6th Airborne Division on the night of June 5/6, in a coup de main operation. The remainder of the division had come by either parachute or glider to the area, where it spent the day defending the bridge, turning back determined German counter-attacks.

There were all kinds of special events at Ranville and at the bridge over the Caen Canal on the 40th anniversary, including an air drop by a platoon of paratroopers from the Parachute Regiment, themselves veterans of Northern Ireland and the Falklands War. Queen Elizabeth II came through the Caen Canal on the royal yacht *Britannia*, passing under the raised bridge and saluting it as she did so.

Obviously, this was no ordinary bridge, and the struggle that took place for control of it was no ordinary battle. Called Pegasus Bridge today, after the symbol of the British airborne forces, the British chose it as the centerpiece of their anniversary celebration because it was an operation that showed the British at their best. Furthermore, it was the critical point on their flank of the invasion.

* * *

Bridges are always central features in war. Battles and campaigns are often decided by who holds the bridge, or seizes the bridge, or destroys the bridge.

In World War II, in the campaign in Northwest Europe, three bridges became especially famous. The first was the Ludendorff Railroad Bridge at Remagen, on the Rhine River. On March 7, 1945, First Lieutenant Karl H. Timmerman rushed his company of the U.S. 9th Armored Division across the bridge, expecting it to be blown at any instant, in the face of enemy fire. It was one of the great actions of the war, and has been appropriately celebrated in books, magazine articles, and movies (the best account is Ken Hechler's *The Bridge at Remagen*).

The second famous bridge was Arnhem. It was better known in the British Isles than in the United States until 1974, when Cornelius Ryan published *A Bridge Too Far*. With that book, the exploits of Colonel John Frost and his paratroopers on the Arnhem Bridge received their proper due on both sides of the Atlantic.

The third bridge, Pegasus, remains better known in the United Kingdom than in the United States, even though it was a featured section of the movie version of Ryan's *The Longest Day* and is covered in every extended account of the invasion. But no book-length account has appeared.

I first became attracted to the story on June 7, 1981. I was at Pegasus Bridge with a group of American veterans and their wives, leading a tour of World War II battlefields. We had examined the bridge, marveled at the skill of the glider pilots, visited the small museum. I had just got the group back on the bus and was ready to move out—behind schedule as always—when a white-haired, exceedingly friendly older man, leaning on a cane, stopped me as I boarded the bus and asked, "I say, are any of you chaps from the British Sixth Airborne Division?"

"No, sir," I replied, "we're all Americans on this bus."

"Oh, I'm sorry," he said.

"Don't be sorry," I answered. "We're all rather proud to be Americans. Were you in the Sixth Airborne?"

"I was indeed," he replied. "I'm Major John Howard."

"How do you do? How do you do?" I exclaimed, pumping his hand. "What a thrill and honor to meet you."

He asked if "my chaps" would like to hear a word or two about what had happened here. Indeed they would, I assured him, and dashed to the bus to get everyone out. We gathered around Major Howard, who stood on the embankment, his back to the bridge. Nearly every one of us on the tour was a hopeless addict for war stories—consequently we were all experts. All of us agreed afterward that never had we heard such good war stories, so well told. The next year, Howard was a featured speaker for my tour group, telling in more detail about the events of June 6, 1944.

He came again in 1983, giving an especially memorable account. As the bus pulled out that year to head for Rommel's headquarters, en route to Paris, he stood in front of the café and snapped into a salute. At that moment, I decided I wanted to write the story of Pegasus Bridge.

I had just completed twenty years of work on Dwight D. Eisenhower. During this time, I had studied something over two million documents before writing a manuscript of more than two thousand pages. I necessarily looked at World War II, and then the Cold War, from the rarefied perspective of the Supreme Commander and the President. In my next book, I wanted to do something radically different, in terms of sources, length, and perspective.

Pegasus fit perfectly. A company in action does not produce much in the way of documentary evidence, but it does create vivid memories—meaning my sources would be interviews with survivors, rather than surviving documents. As to length, one day in the life of one company would obviously be much, much shorter than the seventy-eight years of Ike's life. Finally, Pegasus would let me get down to the level of a company commander and his men, where the action is.

What I had in mind is best said by Russ Weigley in his preface to his magisterial book *Eisenhower's Lieutenants.* Weigley writes, "I have long been troubled by the tendency of the 'new' military history of the post-1945 era . . . to avoid venturing into the heat of battle. This avoidance is in part an effort to generate supposed academic and intellectual respectability for modern military history . . . Nevertheless, it is to prepare for and to wage war that armies primarily exist, and for the military historian to avoid the test of war is to leave his work grotesquely incomplete." After all those years I had spent studying Ike, I felt the force of that passage, because at Ike's level one did not hear the guns, see the dead, feel the fear, know any combat.

Weigley's concluding sentence also intrigued me. He wrote, "A day's trial by battle often reveals more of the essential nature of an army than a generation of peace."

How true, I thought, and I also thought the principle could be extended; one day's trial by battle often reveals more of the essential nature of a people than a generation of peace. Thus one of the most appealing aspects of the story of John Howard and D Company of the Ox and Bucks was the way it revealed the true quality of both the British Army and the British people.

I have always been impressed by the work of S. L. A. Marshall, especially by his use of postcombat interviews to determine what actually happened on the battlefield. Marshall insists that to do the job right, the combat historian must conduct the interviews immediately after the battle. That was obviously impossible, and in any case I felt that for the participants, D-Day was the great day of their lives, stamped forever in their memories. I knew that was the case with Ike, who went on to two full terms as President of the United States, but who always looked back on D-Day as his greatest day, and could remember the most surprising details.

I did the interviews in the fall of 1983, in Canada, England, France, and Germany. I got twenty hours on tape with John Howard, ten hours with Jim Wallwork, five hours with Hans von Luck, two or three hours with the others.

Listening to the old veterans was a fascinating process. D-Day had burned itself indelibly into their minds, and they very much enjoyed having an interested audience for their stories. The major problem with doing a book based solely on interviews, it turned out, was the sequence and timing of events. I would hear six or eight individual descriptions of the same incident. When the veterans differed, it was only in small detail. But they often disagreed on when the specific incident took place, whether it was before this one or after that one. By comparing all the transcripts of the interviews, and by using such documentary material as exists, and by constant rechecking with my sources, I worked out a sequence of events and incidents that is, I think, as close to accurate as one can get forty years later.

The key time, on which everything else hinges, is the moment the first glider crash-landed. I use 0016, D-Day, as that moment, on the basis of John Howard's watch, and the watch of one of the privates. Both stopped at precisely 0016, presumably as a result of the crash.

There will always be controversy over who was the first Allied soldier to touch the soil of France on June 6, 1944. Pathfinders from the U.S. 82d and 101st Airborne, and from the British 6th Airborne, all have claims to the honor. Whether Jim Wallwork, John Howard, and the others in D Company's #1 glider were the absolute first or not is impossible to say. What is absolutely fixed is that D Company of the Ox and Bucks was the first company to go into action as a unit on D-Day. It also had the most demanding and important task of any of the thousands of companies involved in the assault. It carried out its task brilliantly. What follows is the story of how it was done.

1

D-DAY: 0000 TO 0015 HOURS

IT WAS A steel-girder bridge, painted gray, with a large water tower and superstructure. At 0000 hours, June 5/6, 1944, the scudding clouds parted sufficiently to allow the nearly full moon to shine and reveal the bridge, standing starkly visible above the shimmering water of the Caen Canal.

On the bridge, Private Vern Bonck, a twenty-two-year-old Pole conscripted into the German Army, clicked his heels sharply as he saluted Private Helmut Romer, an eighteen-year-old Berliner. Romer had reported to relieve Bonck. As Bonck went off duty, he met with his fellow sentry, another Pole. They decided they were not sleepy and agreed to go to the local brothel, in the village of Bénouville, for a bit of fun. They strolled west along the bridge road, then turned south (left) at the T-junction, and were on the road into Bénouville. By 0005 they were at the brothel. Regular customers, within two minutes they were knocking back cheap red wine with two French whores.

Beside the bridge, on the west bank, south of the road, Georges and Thérèsa Gondrée and their two daughters slept in their small café. They were in separate rooms, not by choice but as a way to use every room and thus to keep the Germans from billeting soldiers with them. It was the 1,450th night of the German occupation of Bénouville.

So far as the Germans knew, the Gondrées were simple Norman peasants, people of no consequence who gave them no trouble. Indeed, Georges sold beer, coffee, food, and a concoction made by Madame of rotting melons and half-fermented sugar to the grateful German troops stationed at the bridge. There were about fifty of them, the NCOs and officers all German, the enlisted men mostly conscripts from Eastern Europe.

But the Gondrées were not as simple as they pretended to be. Madame came from Alsace and spoke German, a fact she successfully hid from the garrison. Georges, before acquiring the café, had been for twelve years a clerk in Lloyd's Bank in Paris and understood English. The Gondrées hated the Germans for what they had done to France, hated the life they led under the occupation, feared for the future of their daughters, and were consequently active in trying to bring German rule to an end. In their case, the most valuable thing they could do for the Allies was to provide information on conditions at the bridge. Thérèsa got information by listening to the chitter-chatter of the NCOs in the café; she passed along to Georges, who passed it to Mme. Vion, director of the maternity hospital, who passed it along to the Resistance in Caen on her trips to the city for medical supplies. From Caen, it was passed on to England via

Lysander airplanes, small craft that could land in fields and get out in a hurry.

Only a few days ago, on June 2, Georges had sent through this process a tidbit Thérèsa had overheard—that the button that would set off the explosives to blow the bridge was located in the machine-gun pillbox across the road from the antitank gun. He hoped that information had got through, if only because he would hate to see his bridge destroyed.

The man who would give that order, the commander of the garrison at the bridge, was Major Hans Schmidt. Schmidt had an understrength company of the 736th Grenadier Regiment of the 716th Infantry Division. At 0000 hours, June 5/6, he was in Ranville, a village two kilometers east of the Orne River. The river ran parallel to the canal, about four hundred meters to the east, and was also crossed by a bridge (fixed, and guarded by sentries but without emplacements or a garrison). Although the Germans expected the long-anticipated invasion at any time, and although Schmidt had been told that the two bridges were the most critical points in Normandy, because they provided the only crossings of the Orne waterways along the Norman coast road, Schmidt did not have his garrison at full alert, nor was he in Ranville on business. Except for the two sentries on each bridge, his troops were either sleeping in their bunkers, or dozing in their slit trenches or in the machine-gun pillbox, or off whoring in Bénouville.

Schmidt himself was with his girl friend in Ranville, enjoying the magnificent food and drink of Normandy. He thought of himself as a fanatic Nazi, this Schmidt, who was determined to do his duty for his Führer. But he seldom let duty interfere with pleasure, and he had no worries that evening. His routine concern was the possibility of French partisans blowing his bridges, but that hardly seemed likely except in conjunction with an airborne operation, and the high winds and stormy weather of the past two days precluded a parachute drop. He had orders to blow the bridges himself if capture seemed imminent. He had prepared the bridges for demolition, but had not put the explosives into their chambers, for fear of accident or the partisans. Since his bridges were almost five miles inland, he figured he would have plenty of warning before any Allied units reached him, even paratroopers, because the paras were notorious for taking a long time to form up and get organized after their drops scattered them all over the DZ. Schmidt treated himself to some more wine, and another pinch.

At Vimont, east of Caen, Colonel Hans A. von Luck, commanding the 125th Panzer Grenadier Regiment of the 21st Panzer Division, was working on personnel reports at his headquarters. The contrast between Schmidt and von Luck extended far beyond their activities at midnight. Schmidt was an officer gone soft from years of cushy occupation duty; von Luck was an officer hardened by combat. Von Luck had been in Poland in 1939, had commanded the leading reconnaissance battalion for Rommel at Dunkirk in 1940, had been in the van at Moscow in 1941 (in December, he actually led his battalion into the outskirts of Moscow, the deepest penetration of the campaign) and with Rommel throughout the North African campaign of 1942–43.

There was an equally sharp contrast between the units von Luck and Schmidt commanded. The 716th Infantry was a second-rate, poorly equipped, immobile division made up of a hodgepodge of Polish, Russian, French, and other conscripted troops, while the 21st Panzer was Rommel's favorite division. Von Luck's regiment, the 125th, was one of the best equipped in the German Army. The 21st Panzer Division had been destroyed in Tunisia in April and May 1943, but Rommel had got most of the officer corps out of the trap, and around that nucleus rebuilt the division. It had all-new equipment, including Tiger tanks, self-propelled vehicles (SPVs) of all types, and an outstanding wireless communications network. The men were volunteers, young Germans deliberately raised by the Nazis for the challenge they were about to face, tough, well trained, eager to come to grips with the enemy.

There was a tremendous amount of air activity that night, with British and American bombers crossing the Channel to bomb Caen. As usual, Schmidt paid no attention to it. Neither did von Luck, consciously, but he was so accustomed to the sights and sounds of combat that at about 0010 hours he noticed something none of his clerks did. There were a half-dozen or so planes flying unusually low, at five hundred feet or less. That could only mean they were dropping something by parachute. Probably supplies for the Resistance, von Luck thought, and he ordered a search of the area, hoping to capture some local resisters while they were gathering in the supplies.

* * *

Heinrich (now Henry) Heinz Hickman, a sergeant in the German 6th (Independent) Parachute Regiment, was at that moment riding in an open staff car, coming from Ouistreham, on the coast, toward Bénouville. Hickman, twenty-four years old, was a combat veteran of Sicily and Italy. His regiment had come to Normandy a fortnight ago; at 2300 hours on June 5 his company commander had ordered Hickman to pick up four young privates at observation posts outside Ouistreham and bring them back to headquarters, near Bréville, on the east side of the river.

Hickman, himself a paratrooper, also heard low-flying planes. He came to the same conclusion as von Luck, that they were dropping supplies to the Resistance, and for the same reason—he could not imagine that the Allies would make a paratrooper drop with only a half-dozen airplanes involved. He drove on toward the bridge over the Caen Canal.

Over the Channel, at 0000 hours, two groups of three Halifax bombers flew at seven thousand feet toward Caen. With all the other air activity going on, neither German searchlights nor AA gunners noticed that each Halifax was tugging a Horsa glider.

Inside the lead glider, Private Wally Parr of D Company, the 2d Oxfordshire and Buckinghamshire Light Infantry (Ox and Bucks), a part of the Air Landing Brigade of the 6th Airborne Division of the British Army, was leading the twenty-eight men in singing. With his powerful voice and strong Cockney accent, Parr was booming out "Abby, Abby, My Boy." Corporal Billy Gray, sitting down the row from Parr, was barely singing, because all that he could think about was the pee he had to take. At the back end of the glider, Corporal Jack Bailey sang, but he also worried about the parachute he was responsible for securing.

The pilot, twenty-four-year-old Staff Sergeant Jim Wallwork, of the Glider Pilot Regiment, anticipated casting off any second now, because he could see the surf breaking over the Norman coast. Beside him his copilot, Staff Sergeant John Ainsworth, was concentrating intensely on his stopwatch. Sitting behind Ainsworth, the commander of D Company, Major John Howard, a thirty-one-year-old former regimental sergeant major and an ex-cop, laughed with everyone else when the song ended and Parr called out, "Has the major laid his kitt yet?" Howard suffered from airsickness and had vomited on every training flight. On this flight, however, he had not been sick. Like his men, he had not been in combat before, but the prospect seemed to calm him more than it shook him.

As Parr started up "It's a Long, Long Way to Tipperary," Howard touched the tiny red shoe in his battle-jacket pocket, one of his two-year-old son Terry's infant shoes that he had brought along for good luck. He thought of Joy, his wife, and Terry and their baby daughter, Penny. They were back in Oxford, living near a factory, and he hoped there were no bombing raids that night. Beside Howard sat Lieutenant Den Brotheridge, whose wife was pregnant and due to deliver any day (five other men in the company had pregnant wives back in England). Howard had talked Brotheridge into joining the Ox and Bucks, and had selected his platoon for the #1 glider because he thought Brotheridge and his platoon the best in his company.

One minute behind Wallwork's glider was #2, carrying Lieutenant David Wood's platoon. Another minute behind that Horsa was #3 glider, with Lieutenant R. "Sandy" Smith's platoon. The three gliders in this group were going to cross the coast near Cabourg, well east of the mouth of the Orne River.

Parallel to that group, to the west and a few minutes behind, Captain Brian Priday sat with Lieutenant Tony Hooper's platoon, followed by the gliders carrying the platoons of Lieutenants H. J. "Tod" Sweeney and Dennis Fox. This second group was headed toward the mouth of the Orne River. In Fox's platoon, Sergeant M. C. "Wagger" Thornton was singing "Cow Cow Boogie" and—like almost everyone else on all the gliders—chain-smoking Players cigarettes.

In #2 glider, with the first group, the pilot, Staff Sergeant Oliver Boland, who had just turned twenty-three years old a fortnight past, found crossing the Channel an "enormously emotional" experience, setting off as he was "as the spearhead of the most colossal army ever assembled. I found it difficult to believe because I felt so insignificant."

At 0007, Wallwork cast off his lead glider as he crossed the coast. At that instant, the invasion had begun.

There were 156,000 men prepared to go into France that day, by air and by sea, British, Canadian, and American, organized into some twelve thousand companies. D Company led the way. It was not only the spearhead of the mighty host, it was also the only company attacking as a completely independent unit. Howard would have no one to report to, or take orders from, until he had completed his principal task. When Wallwork cast off, D Company was on its own.

With cast-off, there was a sudden jerk, then dead silence. Parr and his singers shut up, the engine noise of the bomber faded away, and there was a silence broken only by the swoosh of air over the Horsa's wings. Clouds covered the moon; Ainsworth had to use a flash-light to see his stopwatch, which he had started instantaneously with cast-off.

After casting off, the Halifax bombers continued on toward Caen, where they were to drop their small bomb load on the cement factory, more as a diversion than a serious attack. During the course of the campaign, Caen was almost completely obliterated, with hardly a brick left mortared to a brick. The only untouched building in the whole city was the cement factory. "They were great tug pilots," says Wallwork, "but terrible bombers."

Howard's thoughts shifted from Joy, Penny, and Terry to his other "family," D Company. He thought of how deeply involved he was with his platoon commanders, his sergeants and corporals, and many of his privates. They had been preparing, together, for more than two years for this moment. The officers and men had done all that he asked of them, and more. By God, they were the best damn company in the whole British Army! They had earned this extraordinary role; they deserved it. John was proud of every one of them, and of himself, and he felt a wave of comradeship come over him, and he loved them all.

Then his mind flashed through the dangers ahead.

The antiglider poles, first of all—air-reconnaissance photographs taken in the past few days revealed that the Germans were digging holes for the poles (called "Rommel's asparagus" by the Allies). Were the poles in place or not? Everything depended on the pilots until the instant the gliders had landed, and until that instant Howard was but a passenger. If the pilots could bring D Company down safely, within four hundred meters of the objective, he was confident he could carry out his first task successfully. But if the pilots were even one kilometer off course, he doubted that he could do his job. Any farther than a kilometer and there was no chance. If the Germans somehow spotted the gliders coming in, and got a machine gun on them, the men would never touch the soil of France alive. If the pilots crashed, into a tree, an embankment, or one of Rommel's asparagus, they might all well die even as their feet touched French soil.

Howard was always a bad passenger; he was the type who wanted to drive himself. On this occasion, as he willed Wallwork onto the target, he at least had something physical to do for diversion. Held by a couple of men, Lieutenant Brotheridge began to open the side door. It stuck, and Howard had to help him. Looking down, once the door was open, they could see nothing but cloud. Still, they grinned at each other before slumping back into their seats, recalling the fifty-franc bet they had made as to who would be the first out of the glider.

As he took his seat again, Howard's orders flashed through his mind. Dated May 2, they had been unchanged since. Signed by Brigadier Nigel Poett, and classified "Bigot" (a superclassification, above "Top Secret"; the few who did have clearance for "Bigot" material were said to be "bigoted"), Howard's orders read: "Your task is to seize *intact* the bridges over the River Orne and canal at Bénouville and Ranville, and to hold them until relief . . . The capture of the bridges will be a coup de main operation depending largely on surprise, speed and dash for success. Provided the bulk of your force lands safely, you should have little difficulty in overcoming the known opposition on the bridges. Your difficulties will arise in holding off an enemy counterattack on the bridges, until you are relieved."

The relief would come from the men of the 6th Airborne Division, specifically from the 5th Para Brigade and especially its 7th Battalion. They would land in DZs between the Orne River and the River Dives at 0050 hours. Brigadier Poett, commanding 5th Para Brigade, told Howard that he could expect organized reinforcements within two hours of touchdown. The paras would come through Ranville, where Poett intended to set up his headquarters for the defense of the bridges.

Poett himself was only two or three minutes behind Howard, flying with the pathfinders who would mark the DZ for the main body of the 5th Para Brigade. There were six planes in Poett's group—these were the low-flying planes von Luck and Hickman had heard. Poett wanted to be the first to jump, but at 0008 hours he was struggling desperately to get the floor hatch open. He and his ten men were jammed into an old Albemarle bomber, which none of them had ever seen before. They were carrying so much equipment that they had to "push and push and push to get in." They had then had a terrible time squeezing together sufficiently to close the hatch door. Now, over the Channel with the coast coming up, they could not get the damn thing open. Poett began to fear he would never get out at all, that he would end up landing ignominiously back in England.

In #3 glider, Lieutenant Sandy Smith felt his stomach clinch as it did before a big sports event. He was only twenty-two years old, and he rather liked the feeling of tension, because he was full of the confidence he used to feel before a match when he was a Cambridge rugby star. "We were eager," he remembers, "we were fit. And we were totally innocent. I mean my idea was that everyone was going to be incredibly brave with drums beating and bands playing and I was going to be the bravest among the brave. There was absolutely no doubt at all in my mind that that was going to be the case."

Across the aisle from Smith, Dr. John Vaughan sat fidgeting. He was distinctly unhappy when Smith opened the door. Vaughan was a doctor with the paratroopers, had many jumps behind him, had confidence in a parachute. But he had volunteered for this special mission, not knowing what it was, and ended up in a plywood glider, an open door in front of him, and no parachute. He kept thinking, "My God, why haven't I got a parachute?"

Back in Oxford, Joy Howard slept. She had had a routine day, taking care of Terry and Penny, doing her housework, getting the children into bed at 7 P.M., then spending a couple of hours by the radio, smocking Penny's little dresses.

On his last furlough, John had hidden his dress uniform in a spare-room closet. He had then taken Terry's red baby shoe, kissed the children, started to leave, and returned to kiss them once more. As he left, he told Joy that when she heard that the invasion had started, she could stop worrying, because his job would be finished. Joy had discovered the missing shoe and found the uniform. She knew that the invasion must be imminent, because leaving the uniform behind meant that John did not expect to be dining in the officers' mess for the foreseeable future.

But that had been weeks ago, and nothing had happened since. For two years there had been talk of an invasion, but nothing happened. On June 5, 1944, Joy had no special feelings—she just went to bed. She did hear air traffic, but because most of the bombers based in the Midlands were headed south, rather than east, she was on the fringes of the great air armada and paid little attention to the accustomed noise. She slept.

Down in the southeastern end of London, almost in Kent, Irene Parr did hear and see the huge air fleet headed toward Normandy, and she immediately surmised that the invasion had begun, partly because of the numbers, partly because Wally—in a gross breach of security—had told her that D Company was going to lead the way and he guessed it would be in the first week of June, when the moon was right. She did not know, of course, exactly where he was, but she was sure he was in great danger, and she prayed for him. She would have been pleased, had she known, that Wally's last thoughts, before leaving England, were of her. Just before boarding Wallwork's Horsa, Wally had taken a piece of chalk and christened the glider the "Lady Irene."

Wallwork had crossed the coast well to the east of the mouth of the Orne River. Although he was the pilot of the #1 glider, and #2 and #3 were directly behind him, he was not leading the group to the LZ. Rather, each pilot was on his own, as the pilots could not see the other gliders in any case. Boland remembers the feeling "of being on your own up there, dead quiet, floating over the coast of France, and knowing that there's no turning back."

Wallwork could not see the bridges, not even the river and canal. He was flying by Ainsworth's stopwatch, watching his compass, his airspeed indicator, his altimeter. Three minutes and forty-two seconds into the run, Ainsworth said, "Now!" and Wallwork threw the descending glider into a full right turn.

He looked out the window for a landmark. He could see nothing. "I can't see the Bois de Bavent," he whispered to Ainsworth, not wanting to upset his passengers. Ainsworth snapped back, "For God's sake, Jim, it is the biggest place in Normandy. Pay attention."

"It's not there," Jim whispered fiercely.

"Well, we are on course anyway," Ainsworth replied. Then he started counting: "Five, four, three, two, one, bingo. Right one turn to starboard onto course." Wallwork heaved over the wooden steering wheel and executed another turn. He was now headed north, along the east bank of the canal, descending rapidly. Using the extra-large "barn door" wing flaps, he had brought the glider from seven thousand to about five hundred feet and reduced its airspeed from 160 mph to about 110 mph.

Below and behind him, Caen was ablaze, from tracers shot at bombers and from searchlights and from fires started by the bombers. Ahead of him, he could see nothing. He hoped Ainsworth was right and they were on target.

That target was a small, triangular-shaped field, about five hundred meters long, with the base on the south, the tip near the southeast end of the canal bridge. Wallwork could not see it, but he had studied photographs and a detailed model of the area so long and so hard that he had a vivid mental picture of what he was headed toward.

There was the bridge itself, with its superstructure and water tower at the east end the dominant features of the flat landscape. There was a machine-gun pillbox just north of the bridge, on the east side, and an anti-tank gun emplacement across the road from it. These fortifications were surrounded by barbed wire. At Wallwork's last conference with Howard, Howard had told him that he wanted the nose of the Horsa to break through the barbed wire. Wallwork thought to himself that there was not a chance in hell that he could land that big, heavy, cumbersome, badly overloaded, powerless Horsa with such precision, at midnight, over a bumpy and untested landing strip he could barely see. But out loud he assured Howard he would do his best. What he and Ainsworth thought, however, was that such a sudden stop would result in "a broken leg or so, maybe two each." And they agreed among themselves that if they got out of this caper with only broken legs, they would be lucky.

Along with the constant concern about his location,

and with the intense effort to penetrate the darkness and clouds, Wallwork had other worries. He would be doing between 90 and 100 mph when he hit the ground. If he ran into a tree or an antiglider pole, he would be dead, his passengers too injured or stunned to carry out their task. And the parachute worried him too. It was in the back of the glider, held in place by Corporal Bailey. Wallwork had agreed to add the parachute at the last minute, because his Horsa was so overloaded and Howard refused to remove one more round of ammunition. The idea was that the arrester parachute would provide a safer, quicker stop. What Wallwork feared that it would do was throw him into a nose dive.

The control mechanism for the chute was over Ainsworth's head. At the proper moment, he would press an electric switch and the trapdoor would fall open, the chute billow out. When Ainsworth pressed another switch, the chute would fall away from the glider. Wallwork understood the theory; he just hoped he would not have to use the chute in fact.

At 0014 Wallwork called over his shoulder to Howard to get ready. Howard and the men linked arms and brought their knees up. Most everyone thought the obvious thoughts—"No turning back now," or "Here we go," or "This is it." Howard recalled, "I could see ole Jim holding that bloody great machine and driving it in at the last minute, the look on his face was one that one could never forget. I could see those damn great footballs of sweat across his forehead and all over his face."

Gliders #2 and #3 were directly behind Wallwork, at their one-minute intervals. The other group of Horsas was, however, now split up. Priday's #4 glider had gone up the River Dives rather than the Orne River. Seeing a bridge over the Dives at about the right distance inland, the pilot of #4 glider was preparing to land. The other two Horsas, on the correct course, headed up the Orne River. They had a straight-in run. They would "prang," a gliderman's term for touch-down, pointed south, along the west bank of the river, in a rectangular field nearly one thousand meters long.

Brigadier Poett finally got his hatch open (in another of those Albemarles one of Poett's officers fell out while opening his hatch and was lost in the Channel). Standing over the hole in the floor of the bomber, a foot on each side, Poett could not see anything. He flew right over the Merville Battery, another critical target for the paras that night. Another minute and it was 0016 hours. The pilot flipped on the green light, and Poett brought his feet together and fell through the hatch into the night.

On the canal bridge, Private Romer and the other sentry were putting in another night of routine pacing back and forth across the bridge. The bombing activity at Caen was old stuff to them, not their responsibility and not worth a glance. The men in the machine-gun pillbox dozed, as usual, as did the troops standing to in the slit trenches. The antitank gun was unmanned.

In Ranville, Major Schmidt opened another bottle of wine. In Bénouville, Private Bonck had finished his wine and had gone into the bedroom with his little French whore. He unbuckled his belt and began to unbutton his trousers as the whore slipped out of her dress. On the road from Ouistreham, Sergeant Hickman and his group in the staff car sped south, toward Bénouville and the bridge. At the café, the Gondrées slept.

Wallwork was down to two hundred feet, his airspeed slightly below 100 mph. At 0015 he was halfway down the final run. About two kilometers from his target, the clouds cleared the moon. Wallwork could see the river and the canal—they looked like strips of silver to him. Then the bridge loomed before him, exactly where he expected it. "Well," he thought to himself, "I gotcha now."

2

D-DAY MINUS TWO YEARS

SPRING 1942 WAS a bad time for the Allies. In North Africa, the British were taking a pounding. In Russia, the Germans had launched a gigantic offensive aimed at Stalingrad. In the Far East, the Japanese had over-run the American, British, and Dutch colonial possessions and were threatening Australia. In France, and throughout Western and Eastern Europe, Hitler was triumphant. The only bright spot was that the previous December 7, America had entered the war. But to date that event had produced only a few more ships, and no troops, no planes, hardly even an increased flow of lend-lease supplies.

Throughout the British Army, nevertheless, boredom reigned. The so-called phony war was from September of 1939 to May of 1940, but for thousands of young men who had enlisted during that period, the time from spring 1941 to the beginning of 1944 was almost as bad. There was no threat of invasion. The only British army doing any fighting at all was in the Mediterranean; almost everywhere else, duties and training were routine—and routinely dull. Discipline had fallen off, in part because of the boredom, in part because the War Office had concluded that martinet discipline in a democracy was inappropriate, and because it was thought it dampened the fighting spirit of the men in the ranks.

Many soldiers, obviously, rather enjoyed this situation and would have been more than content to stick out the war lounging around barracks, doing the odd parade or field march, otherwise finding ways of making it look as if they were busy. But there were thousands who were not content, young men who had joined up because they really did want to be soldiers, really did want to fight for King and Country, really did seek some action and excitement. In the spring of 1942, their opportunity came when a call went out for volunteers for the airborne forces.

Britain had made a decision to create an airborne army. The 1st Airborne Division was being formed up. Major General F. A. M. "Boy" Browning would command it. Already a legendary figure in the Army, noted especially for his tough discipline, Browning looked like a movie star and dressed with flair. In 1932 he had married the novelist Daphne du Maurier, who in 1942 suggested a red beret for airborne troops, with Bellerophon astride winged Pegasus as the airborne shoulder patch and symbol.

Wally Parr was one of the thousands who responded to the call to wear the red beret. He had joined the Army in February 1939, at the age of sixteen (he was one of more than a dozen in D Company, Ox and Bucks, who lied about his age to enlist). He had been posted to an infantry regiment and had spent three years "never doing a damn thing that really mattered. Putting up barbed wire, taking it down the next day, moving it. . . . Never fired a rifle, never did a thing." So he volunteered for airborne, passed the physical, and was accepted into the Ox and Bucks, just then forming up as an air landing unit, and was assigned to D Company. After three days in his new outfit, he asked for an interview with the commander, Major John Howard.

"Ah, yes, Parr," Howard said as Parr walked into his office. "What can I do for you?"

"I want to get out," Parr stated.

Howard stared at him. "But you just got in."

"Yeah, I know," Parr responded, "and I spent the last three days weeding around the barracks block. That's not what I came for. I want to transfer from here to the paras. I want the real thing, what I volunteered for, not these stupid gliders, of which we don't have any anyway."

"You take it easy," Howard replied. "Wait." And he dismissed Parr without another word.

Leaving the office, Parr thought, "I'd better be careful with this fellow."

In truth, Parr as yet had no idea just how tough his new company commander was. Howard had come out of a background that was as working class as any of the Cockneys in his company. Born December 8, 1912, he was the eldest of nine children. From the time John was two years old until he was six, his father, Jack Howard, was off in France, fighting the Great War. When Jack returned, he got a job with Courage's brewery, making barrels. The family lived in the West End of London, where John's mother, Ethel, a dynamic woman, managed to keep them in clean clothes and adequately fed. John recalls, "I spent the best part of my childhood, up to the age of thirteen or fourteen, pushing prams, helping out with the shopping, and doing all that sort of thing."

John's one great pleasure in life was the Boy Scouts. The Scouts got him out of London for weekend camps, and in the summer he would get a fortnight's camp somewhere in the country. His chums on the streets of London did not approve; they made fun of his short pants "and generally made my life hell." Not even his younger brothers would stick with the Scouts. But John did. He loved the outdoor life, the sports, and the competition.

John's other great passion was school. He was good at his studies, especially mathematics, and won a scholarship to secondary school. But the economic situation was such that he had to go to work, so he passed up the scholarship and instead, at age fourteen, took a full-time job as a clerk with a broker's firm. He also took evening classes, five nights a week, in English, math, accounting, economics, typing, shorthand, anything that he thought would be beneficial to his work. But in the summer of 1931, when he returned to London from Scout camp, he discovered that his firm had been hammered on the stock exchange and he was out of a job.

By this time the younger Howard children were growing, taking up more space, and the house was bursting. John offered to move out, to find a flat and a job of his own. His mother would not hear of his breaking up the family. So he decided to run off and enlist in the Army.

He went into the King's Shropshire Light Infantry.

The older soldiers, Howard found, were "very rough and tough . . . I freely admit I cried my eyes out for the first couple of nights when I was in the barracks room with these toughs and wondered if I'd survive."

In fact, he began to stand out. In recruit training, at Shrewsbury, he was outstanding in sports—cross-country running, swimming, boxing, all things he had done in the Scouts. To his great benefit the British Army of 1932, like most peacetime regular armies everywhere, was fanatic about sports competition between platoons, companies, battalions. When John joined his battalion, at Colchester, the commanding officer immediately made him the company clerk, a cushy job that left him with plenty of free time to excel in sports. Then he was sent to an education course, to learn to teach, and when he returned he was put to teaching physical education to recruits, and to competing for his company in various events.

That was all right, but John's ambitions reached higher. He decided to try for a commission, based on his sports record, his education qualifications—all those night courses—and his high scores on army exams. But getting a commission from the ranks of the peacetime Army was well-nigh impossible, and he was turned down. He did get a promotion to corporal.

And he met Joy Bromley. It was on a blind date. He had been dragged along because his buddy had two girls to look after. Joy was supposed to be his buddy's date, but John took one look at her and lost his heart forever. Joy was only sixteen (she lied and told John she was eighteen), slim but with a handsome figure, pert in her face, lively in her carriage, quick to laugh, full of conversation. She had come reluctantly on the date—her people were in the retail trade, respectable middle class; she had already been dating a boy from Cambridge; and as she told her friend, "I'm not allowed to go out with soldiers."

"Well, it's only for coffee," her friend persisted, "and I've made a promise." So Joy went, and over the coffee she and John talked, the words, the laughs, the stories bubbling out. At the train station, John kissed her good night.

That was in 1936, and a courtship ensued. At first it was secretive, Joy fearing her mother's disapproval. They met under a large copper beech tree at the foot of the garden at Joy's house. John did not much care for this sneaking around, however, and he decided to proceed on a direct line. He announced to Joy that he was going to see her mother. "Well, I nearly died," Joy recalled. "I thought Mother wouldn't see him," and if she did, then "she would flail me for making such an acquaintance." But Mother—and John—came through splendidly, Mother liking John immediately and telling Joy, "You've got a real man there." In April 1938, they were engaged, promising Joy's mother they would wait until Joy was older before marrying.

In 1938, John's enlistment came to an end. In June, he joined the Oxford City Police force. After a tough and extended training course, in which he came in second out of two hundred, he began walking the streets of Oxford at night. He found it "quite an experience. You are on your own, you know, anything can happen."

* * *

He stayed with the police until after the war began. On October 28, 1939, he and Joy were married. On December 2, he reported for duty as a full corporal with the King's Shropshire Light Infantry. Within two weeks he was a sergeant. One month later he was company sergeant major. In April, he became regimental sergeant major. So he jumped from corporal to regimental sergeant major in five months, something of a record even in wartime. And in May, his brigadier offered him a chance at a commission.

He hesitated. Being regimental sergeant major meant being the top man, responsible only to the commanding officer, the real backbone of the regiment. Why give that up to be a subaltern? Further, as Howard explained to his wife, he did not have a very high opinion of the incoming second lieutenants and did not think he wanted to be a part of them. Joy brushed all his objections aside and told him that he absolutely must try for the commission. Her reaction ended his hesitancy, and he went off to OCTU—Officer Cadet Training Unit—in June 1940.

Upon graduation, he requested the Ox and Bucks, because he liked the association with Oxford and he liked light infantry. Within a fortnight he feared he had made a terrible mistake. The Ox and Bucks were "a good county regiment" with a full share of battle honors, at Bunker Hill, in the Peninsula, at the Battle of New Orleans, Waterloo, and in the Great War. Half the regiment had just come back from India. All the officers came from the upper classes. It was in the nature of things for them to be snobbish, especially to a working-class product who had been a cop and had come up from the ranks. In brief, the officers cut Howard. They meant it to be sharp and cruel, and it was, and it hurt.

After two weeks of the silent treatment, Howard phoned Joy, then living with her family in Shropshire. "You'd better plan to move here," he declared. "Because it's just horrible and I need some encouragement or I am not going to stick it. I don't have to put up with this." Joy promised him she would move quickly.

The following morning, on the parade ground, Howard was putting four squads through a drill. He already had his men sharp enough to do some complicated maneuvers. When he dismissed the squads, he turned to see his colonel standing behind him. In a quiet voice, the colonel asked, "Why don't you bring your wife here, Howard?" Within a week, Joy had found a flat in Oxford and John had been accepted by his fellow officers.

Soon he was a captain with his own company, which he trained for the next year. At the beginning of 1942, he learned that a decision had been taken to go airborne with the Ox and Bucks, and that his battalion would be gliderborne troops. No one was forced to go airborne; every officer and trooper was given a choice. About 40 percent declined the opportunity to wear the red beret. Another 10 percent were weeded out in the physical exam. It was meant to be an elite regiment.

The sergeant major came to the Ox and Bucks specially posted from the outside. Wally Parr makes the man's overpowering personality vivid in a short anecdote. "That first day," says Parr, "he called the whole bleeding regiment together on parade. And he looked at us, and we looked at him, and we both knew who was boss."

Howard himself had to give up his company and his

captaincy to go airborne, but he did not hesitate. He reverted to lieutenant and platoon leader in order to become an airborne officer. In three weeks, his colonel promoted him and gave him command of D Company. Shortly after that, in May of 1942, he was promoted to major.

D Company as noted, came half from the original Ox and Bucks, half from volunteers drawn from every branch of the Army. The men came from all over the United Kingdom, and from every class and occupation. What they had in common was that they were young, fit, eager to be trained, ready for excitement, the kind of troops every company commander wishes he could have.

Howard's platoon leaders also came from different backgrounds. Two were Cambridge students when they volunteered, one was a graduate of the University of Bristol, but the oldest lieutenant, at age twenty-six, was Den Brotheridge, who, like Howard, had come up from the ranks. Indeed, Howard had originally recommended Den, then a corporal, for OCTU. His fellow platoon leaders were a bit uneasy about Den when he first joined up; as one of them explained, "He wasn't one of us, you know." Den played soccer rather than rugby and cricket. But, the officer immediately added, "You couldn't help but like him." Den was a first-class athlete, good enough that it was freely predicted he would become a professional soccer player after the war.

Captain Brian Priday was Howard's second-in-command. Six feet tall, a quiet, steady type, Priday was ideal for the job. He and Howard hit it off, helped by the fact that Priday's father had also been on the Oxford police force. Priday himself had been in the automobile trade. He was in his mid-twenties. Lieutenants Tod Sweeney and Tony Hooper were in their early twenties; Lieutenant David Wood was all of nineteen years old, fresh out of OCTU. "My gracious," Howard thought to himself when Wood reported, "he is going to be a bit too young for the toughies in my company." But, Howard added, "David was so keen and bubbling with enthusiasm I thought, Well, we've got to make something of him. So I gave him a young soldier platoon with mature NCOs and it worked out fine."

Sweeny describes himself and his fellow subalterns: "We were irresponsible young men, life was very lighthearted, there was a war on, lots of fun for us. John was a dedicated and serious trainer and we were rather like young puppies and he was trying to train us."

Howard was pleased with his company, officers and men. He especially liked having so many Londoners in it. The regiment moved to Bulford. D Company went into a spider block, near the barracks but separate from it. So, Howard notes, "Right from the first there was an atmosphere of D Company being on its own." He set out to make it into a family and into a first-class combat unit.

In North Africa, Hans von Luck was fighting in the only war he ever enjoyed. He commanded the armed reconnaissance battalion on Rommel's extreme right (southern) flank. He thus enjoyed a certain independence, as did his British opposite number. The two commanding officers agreed to fight a civilized war. Every day at 5 P.M. the war shut down, the British to brew up their tea, the Germans their coffee. At about quarter past five, von Luck and the British commander would communicate over the radio. "Well," von Luck might say, "we captured so-and-so today, and he's fine, and he sends his love to his mother, tell her not to worry." Once von Luck learned that the British had received a month's supply of cigarettes. He offered to trade a captured officer—who happened to be the heir to the Players cigarette fortune—for one million cigarettes. The British countered with an offer of 600,000. Done, said von Luck. But the Players heir was outraged. He said the ransom was insufficient. He insisted he was worth the million and refused to be exchanged.

One evening, an excited corporal reported that he had just stolen a British truck jammed with tinned meat and other delicacies. Von Luck looked at his watch—it was past 6 P.M.—and told the corporal he would have to take it back, as he had captured it after 5 P.M. The corporal protested that this was war and anyway the troops were already gathering in the goods from the truck. Von Luck called Rommel, his mentor in military academy. He said he was suspicious of British moves farther south and thought he ought to go out on a two-day reconnaissance. Could another battalion take his place for that time? Rommel agreed. The new battalion arrived in the morning. That night, at 5:30 P.M., just as von Luck had anticipated, the British stole *two* supply trucks.

Heinz Hickman, meanwhile, had gone through the campaigns of 1940 in Holland, Belgium, and France as a gunner on an 88-mm gun. In 1941, he volunteered for the parachute regiment, looking for adventure, and went to Spandau for jump school. In May 1942, he was in the middle of his training.

In Warsaw, Vern Bonck was doing his best to stay out of the German conscription net by working with extra efficiency at his lathe. Helmut Romer, in Berlin, sixteen years old, was finishing his school year.

At the bridge over the Caen Canal, there were as yet no elaborate defenses, and only a tiny garrison. Still, the garrison was large enough to make the lives of the people of Bénouville, Le Port, and Ranville miserable. The Germans helped themselves to the best of everything, paid for what they did purchase with nearly worthless printing-press francs, took all the young men away for slave labor, made travel even within the country almost impossible, imposed a curfew, and shot dissenters. By May 1942, the Gondrées had decided to do something about it. Georges joined the local Resistance, which advised him to stay put and use his situation to get information on the bridges and their defense to the British. As noted, he did so on the basis of his wife's reports on what she heard in the café. Let there be no mistake about this action—the Gondrées knew that if the Germans caught them they would be tortured, then hanged. But they persisted.

In May 1942, Jim Wallwork, a Manchester lad who had volunteered for the Army at age nineteen in March 1939, was also in training camp. Jim's father, who had been an artilleryman in the Great War, had advised him, "Whatever you do, Jim, don't for God's sake join the infantry. Get in the artillery, the biggest gun you can find; if possible, the railway gun." Naturally, Jim ended up in the infantry, bored to tears, although he did make it to sergeant. He tried to transfer out, into the Royal Air Force, but his commanding officer blocked the move because he wanted to keep Wallwork with him.

Then in early 1942 a call went out for volunteers for the Glider Pilot Regiment. Jim signed up, and by spring was at Tilshead, Salisbury Plain, in training. "It was rather rough," he recalled, "because I was doing my own equipment, polishing my own brass, going on those God-awful run-marches, and drills, and all sorts of that nonsense." What he most feared, what every man in the Glider Pilot Regiment most feared, were the letters "RTU." They stood for Return to Unit, disgraced, a failure. Jim managed to stick it, and by May 1942, he was at flight training school, learning to fly a small airplane.

Howard's own family was growing. Joy was then living with relatives near Shrewsbury. She was pregnant. During the war, Howard was a virtual teetotaler, partly because he wanted to keep a clear mind, partly because "I saw the mess a lot of people were getting into, making bloody fools of themselves, and I wanted to set an example for my own subalterns." The child was due in late June; during the fortnight between the due date and the actual delivery, Howard was so irritable and bad-tempered that his subalterns found him unapproachable. On July 12, a son, Terry, was born. When news of the successful delivery arrived in Bulford, everyone was so relieved that a huge party developed. Howard, drinking straight shots of whiskey, "to wet the baby's head," got royally drunk.

* * *

By July, Howard was pretty much on his own, allowed by his colonel to set his own training pace and schedule. Initially, he put the emphasis on teaching the men the skills of the light infantryman. He taught them to be marksmen with their rifles, with the light machine gun, with the carbine and the pistol, with the Piat and other antitank weapons. He instructed them in the many types of grenades, their characteristics and special uses.

The basic weapons of a gliderborne platoon of thirty men included the Enfield .303 rifle, the Sten carbine, the Bren light machine gun, 2-inch and 3-inch mortars, and the Piat (projector infantry antitank). The Enfield was the old reliable British rifle. One or two men in each squad were snipers, equipped with a telescopic sight for their rifles. The Sten was a 9-mm submachine gun that reflected Britain's inability to produce quality weapons for its troops. The Sten was mass-produced, and distributed to thousands of fighting men, not because it was any good, but because it was cheap. It could be fired single shot or automatic, but the weapon frequently jammed and too often it went off on its own. In 1942 David Wood shot Den Brotheridge in the leg with his Sten, after forgetting to put the safety back on. Brotheridge recovered, and indeed he, like all the officers, carried the Sten by choice. It weighed only seven pounds, was only thirty inches long, had an effective range of one hundred yards, and used a box magazine holding thirty-two rounds. For all its short-comings, it was deadly in close-in combat—if it worked.

The Bren gun was a light machine gun, weighing twenty-three pounds, fired either from the hip or from a bipod or a tripod. It had an effective range of five hundred yards and a rate of fire of 120 rounds per minute. There was one Bren gunner per squad; everyone in the squad helped carry the thirty-round magazines. In rate of fire, in dependability, and by other measurements, the Bren was inferior to its German counterpart, the MG 34, just as the Sten was inferior to the German Schmeisser.

The Piat was a hand-held rocket launcher, fired from the shoulder, that threw a three-pound grenade through a barrel at about three hundred feet per second. The hollow-charged grenade would explode on target on impact. Effective range was supposed to be one hundred yards, but the men of D Company never could get more than fifty yards out of the Piat. Being spring-loaded, Piats were inaccurate and subject to frequent jamming. No one liked them very much, but all got proficient with them. Their only other antitank weapon was the Gammon bomb, a plastic explosive charge developed from the "sticky bomb," which could be thrown at a tank and, if all went well, would cling to the tank before exploding.

Most of all, Howard put the emphasis on learning to think quickly. They were elite, he told the men; they were gliderborne troops, and wherever and whenever it was they attacked the enemy, they could be sure the premium would be on quick thinking and quick response.

Howard's emphasis on technical training went a bit beyond what the other company commanders were doing, but only just a bit. Each of Howard's associates were commanding top-quality volunteers, and were volunteers themselves, outstanding officers. What was different about D Company was its commander's mania for physical fitness. It went beyond anything anyone in the British Army had ever seen before. The regiment prided itself on being fit (one officer from B Company described himself as a physical-fitness fanatic), but all were amazed by, and a bit critical of, the way Howard pushed his fitness program.

D Company's day began with a five-mile cross-country run, done at a seven- or eight-minute-to-the-mile pace. After that the men dressed, policed the area, ate breakfast, and then spent the day on training exercises, usually strenuous. In the late afternoon, Howard insisted that everyone engage in some sport or another. His own favorites were the individual endeavors, cross-country running, swimming, and boxing, but he encouraged soccer, rugby, and any sport that would keep his lads active until bedtime.

Those were regular days. Twice a month, Howard would take the whole company out for two or three days, doing field exercises, sleeping rough. He put them through grueling marches, until they became an outstanding marching unit. Wally Parr swears—and a number of his comrades back him up—that they could do twenty-two miles, in full pack, including the Brens and the mortars, in five and one-half hours. When they got back from such a march, Parr relates, "you would have a foot inspection, get a bite to eat, and then in the afternoon face a choice: either play soccer or go for a cross-country run."

All the officers, including Howard, did everything the men did. All of them had been athletes themselves, and loved sports and competition. The sports and the mutually endured misery on the forced marches were bringing officers and men closer together. David Wood was exceedingly popular with his platoon, as was Tod Sweeney, in his own quiet way, with his. But Brotheridge stood out. He played the men's game, soccer, and as a former corporal himself he had no sense of being ill at ease among the men. He would go into their barracks at night, sit on the bed of his batman, Billy Gray, and talk soccer with the lads. He got to bringing his boots along, and shining them as he talked. Wally Parr never got over the sight of a British lieutenant polishing his boots himself while his batman lay back on his bed, gassing on about Manchester United and West Ham and other soccer teams.

Howard's biggest problem was boredom. He racked his brains to find different ways of doing the same things, to put some spontaneity into the training. His young heroes had many virtues, but patience was not one of them. The resulting morale problem extended far beyond D Company, obviously, and in late summer 1942, General Browning sent the whole regiment to Devonshire for two months of cliff climbing. He then decided to march the regiment back to Bulford, some 130 miles. Naturally, it would be a competition between the companies.

The first two days were the hottest of the summer, and the men were marching in serge, wringing wet. After the second day, they pleaded for permission to change to lighter gear. It was granted, and over the next two days a cold, hard rain beat down on their inadequately covered bodies.

Howard marched up and down the column, urging his men on. He had a walking stick, an old army one with an inch of brass on the bottom. His company clerk and wireless operator, Corporal Tappenden, offered the major the use of his bike. "Not likely," Howard growled. "I'm leading my company." His hands grew more blisters than Tappenden's feet, from his grip on the stick, and he wore away all the brass on the end of it. But he kept marching.

On the morning of the fourth day, when Howard roused the men and ordered them to fall in, Wally Parr and his friend Jack Bailey waddled out on their knees. When Howard asked them what they thought they were doing, Wally replied that he and Jack had worn away the bottom half of their legs. But they got up and marched. "Mad bastard," the men whispered among themselves after Howard had moved off. "Mad, ambitious bastard. He'll get us all killed." But they marched.

They got back to base on the evening of the fifth day. They marched in at 140 steps to the minute, singing loudly "Onward, Christian Soldiers." They came in first in the regiment, by half a day. Only two of Howard's men, out of 120, had dropped out of the march. (His stick, however, was so worn he had to throw it away.)

Howard had radioed ahead, and had hot showers and meals waiting for the men. As the officers began to undress for their showers, Howard told them to button up. They had to go do a foot inspection of the men, then watch to make sure they all showered properly, check on the quality and quantity of their food, and inspect the barracks to see that the beds were ready. By the time the officers got to shower, the hot water was gone; by the time they got to eat, only cold left-overs remained. But not one of them had let Howard down.

"From then on," Howard recalls, "we didn't follow the normal pattern of training." His colonel gave him even more flexibility, and the transport to make it meaningful. Howard started taking his company to Southampton, or London, or Portsmouth, to conduct street-fighting exercises in the bombed-out areas. There were plenty to choose from, and it did not matter how much damage D Company did, so all the exercises were with live ammunition.

Howard was putting together an outstanding light-infantry company.

3

D-DAY MINUS ONE YEAR TO D-DAY MINUS ONE MONTH

BY THE SPRING of 1943, the British airborne force had grown sufficiently to divide it into two divisions. The 1st Airborne went off to North Africa. The 6th Airborne Division (the number was chosen to confuse German intelligence) was formed around the companies that stayed behind, including D Company.

General Richard Gale, known to everyone as "Windy," because of his last name, commanded the 6th Airborne Division. A large, confident, experienced officer who had commanded the 1st Para Brigade, Gale had a bit of the buccaneer about him, and more than a bit of imagination to complement his professionalism.

Nigel Poett commanded the 5th Para Brigade. He was a regular officer from the Durham Light Infantry. A big, powerful man, Poett was meticulous on detail and an officer who led from the front. The 3d Para Brigade was commanded by James Hill, a regular from the Royal Fusiliers who had won a DSO in North Africa. D Company was part of the Air Landing Brigade, commanded by Hugh Kindersley.

Under Gale's prodding, training intensified, but there were few complaints, because the word was that the division was being prepared for the invasion of France. Gale, through his training exercises, was trying to figure out what the division was capable of performing, while simultaneously trying to figure out exactly how he would use it to achieve his D-Day objectives.

At COSSAC (Chief of Staff, Supreme Allied Commander), planning for Gale's role, and for the invasion as a whole, had been going on for a year, under the direction of General Frederick Morgan. By the spring of 1943, Morgan and his planners had settled on Normandy, west of the mouth of the Orne River, as the invasion site. A variety of factors influenced the choice; the one that affected D Company and the 6th Airborne Division was the need to protect the left flank of the seaborne invasion, where the British 3d Division would be landing on Sword Beach. That left flank was the single most vulnerable point in the whole invasion, because to the east, beyond Le Havre and the mouth of the Seine River, the Germans had the bulk of their armor in the West. If Rommel brought that armor across the Seine, crossed the River Dives and the Orne River, then launched an all-out counterattack against the exposed flank of 3d Division, he might well roll up the entire invading force, division by division. It would take days for the Allies to unload enough tanks and artillery of their own to withstand such a blow.

Morgan and his people decided to meet the threat by

placing the 6th Airborne between the Orne waterways and the River Dives. There were many changes in the COSSAC plan after January 1944, when Eisenhower took over SHAEF (Supreme Headquarters, Allied Expeditionary Force) and Montgomery took over at 21st Army Group, which commanded all the ground forces; the most important change was the widening of the assault area from three to five divisions. But one COSSAC decision that remained unchanged was the one that placed 6th Airborne on its own, east of the Orne River, with the task of holding off armored counterattacks. How to do it was left to General Gale.

D Company had begun its flight training, in little Waco gliders that carried seven men. Howard concentrated on exit drill. The door was open before the glider touched down; it was "Move, move, move" when the glider hit the ground. Again and again Howard reminded the men that they were "rats in the trap" so long as they were inside.

The chief novelty of flying in a glider was one Howard could not get over. As General Sir Napier Crookenden writes in *Drop Zone Normandy*, "Since the glider on the end of its tug-rope moved in a series of surges as the tug-rope tightened and slackened, and was subject to the normal pitching, rolling and yawing of any aircraft, few men survived more than half-an-hour without being sick. The floor was soon awash with vomit, and this in itself was enough to defeat the strongest stomach." Howard could not get away from being sick; he threw up on all twelve of his training flights. Fortunately, for him it was not like being sea-sick, with its long recovery time. After being sick on a glider flight, Howard was fit and ready as soon as his feet hit the ground.

Howard's sickness gave the men a great laugh, something the company badly needed, as it was in danger of going stale. In barracks, Wally Parr relates, "We would be sleeping, midnight, and all of a sudden the door burst open and in would come a load of screaming maniacs from Sweeney's platoon, throw the beds up in the air, the whole lot. I'm talking about cannon crackers that we used to use for exercises and that, just throwing them about the place, left, right, smoke stuff, a lot of it. It was sheer vitality coupled with total frustration."

Parr, by this time a corporal in charge of the snipers, could not stand the boredom any longer. "Me and Billy Gray and another fellow was bored one night so we decided, just for the fun of it, we'd go and rob the NAAFI*; so we waited until it was pretty dark and then we drifted off to sleep and forgot it, then we woke up about five o'clock and thought, ah, hell, we might as well, so we went over and we broke into the NAAFI and we emptied it of soap, soap powder and everything and came back with it in sackfuls, which we spread all over the cobblestones and pavement. A nice rain stirred it up. You've never seen so much soap in all your life. Everything was foam."

Howard busted Wally back to private and sentenced him to a fortnight in jail; he put Billy Gray and the other lad in jail for twenty-eight days.

Howard's colonel, Mike Roberts, wanted to RTU Private Parr. Howard protested that the punishment was

* The British equivalent of an American PX. The letters stand for Navy, Army, Air Force Institute.

excessive, and in any case told Roberts, "Parr might only be a private but he is the man that when I get to the other side will be promoted straightaway; he is a born leader." Roberts let Howard keep Parr. There were a number of similar outbursts; Howard called the perpetrators "my scallywags" and says, "All the scallywags, when we got to the other side, they were the best. In battle they were in their natural environment. Unfortunately, most of them were killed because of their nature and their way of going about things." He did re-promote Parr on D-Day plus two.

Howard's solution for boredom was to keep the men physically exhausted. He drove himself hardest of all. He would go for long periods with only two or three hours' sleep per day, preparing himself for what he anticipated would be a major problem in combat, the making of quick decisions with an exhausted mind.

Howard also set out, on his own, to make D Company into a first-class night-fighting unit. It was not that he had any inkling that he might be landing at night, but rather he reckoned that once in combat, his troops would be spending a good deal of their time fighting at night. He was also thinking of a favorite expression in the German Army that he had heard: "The night is the friend of no man." In the British Army, the saying was that "the German does not like to fight at night."

The trouble was, neither did the British. Howard decided to deal with the problem of fighting in unaccustomed darkness by turning night into day. He would rouse the company at 2000 hours, take the men for their run, get them fed, and then begin twelve hours of field exercises, drill, the regular paper work—everything that a company in training does in the course of a day. After a meal at 1000 hours, he would get them going on the athletic fields. At 1300 hours he sent them to barracks to sleep. At 2000 hours, they were up again, running. This would go on for a week at a time at first; by early 1944, as Parr recalls, "We went several weeks, continuous weeks of night into day and every now and then he would have a change-around week." And Parr describes the payoff: "Oh, we were used to it, we got quite used to operating in nighttime, doing everything in the dark."

D Company was developing a feeling of independence and separateness. All the sports fanaticism had produced, as Howard had hoped it would, an extreme competitiveness. The men wanted D Company to be first in everything, and they had indeed won the regimental prizes in boxing, swimming, cross-country, soccer, and other sports. When Brigadier Kindersley asked to observe a race among the best runners in the brigade, D Company had entered twenty runners, and took fifteen of the first twenty places. According to Howard, Kindersley "was just cock-a-hoop about it."

That was exactly the response Howard and his company had been working so hard for so long to get. The ultimate competitiveness would come against the Germans, of course, but next best was competing against the other companies. D Company wanted to be first among all the gliderborne companies, not just for the thrill of victory, but because victory in this contest meant a unique opportunity to be a part of history. No one could guess what it might be, but even the lowest private could figure out that the War Office was not going to spend all that money building an elite force and then not use it in the invasion. It was equally obvious that airborne troops would be at the van, almost certainly behind enemy lines—thus a heroic adventure of unimaginable dimensions. And, finally, it was obvious that the best company would have the leading role at the van. That was the thought that sustained Howard and his company through the long dreary months, now stretching into two years, of training.

That thought sustained them because, whether consciously or subconsciously, to a man they were aware that D-Day would be the greatest day of their lives. Nothing that had happened before could possibly compare to, while nothing that happened afterward could possibly match, D-Day. D Company continued to work at a pace that bordered on fanaticism in order to earn the right to be the first to go.

By spring 1943, Jim Wallwork had completed his glider pilot training, using mainly Hotspurs, in the process surviving a grueling course that less than one-third of the volunteers passed. After graduation, Wallwork and his twenty-nine fellow pilots went to Brize Norton, an old peacetime airdrome, "and that is where we saw our first wheel glider, which was the Horsa, and we immediately fell in love with it."

The Horsa was a product of Britain's total war effort. In December 1940, the Air Ministry, responding to the need to conserve critical metals and the need to draw the woodworking industries into wartime production, ordered an all-wooden glider. The prototypes were built at what is now Heathrow Airport; five more were built at Airspeed's Portsmouth works, which went on to build seven hundred production models. It must have been the most wooden aircraft ever built; even the controls in the cockpit were masterpieces of the woodworker's artistry. It was a high-wing monoplane with a large Plexiglas nose and a tricycle landing gear. Wingspan was eighty-eight feet and fuselage length was sixty-seven feet. It could carry a pilot and a co-pilot, plus twenty-eight fully armed men, or two jeeps, or a 75-mm howitzer, or a quarter-ton truck.

So much for the bare facts. Now let Wallwork describe his reaction the first time he saw a Horsa: "We were astonished at the size to start with. It was like a big, black crow. When we first got in, before we ever flew and felt the controls, saw the size of the flaps, we were very impressed, particularly so since we were going to have to fly it." The seats in the cockpit were side-by-side "and very big." Visibility through the front and side was excellent. Each pilot had proper dual controls. The instruments included an airspeed indicator, a turn-and-bank indicator, air-pressure gauge, compass, and altimeter.

"Flying a glider," according to Wallwork, "is just like flying an aircraft. The instruments and controls are the same; the only thing that is short in the glider is the rev count and the temperature gauge. Really, flying a glider on tow is just the same as flying an aircraft except that the engine is a hundred yards ahead and someone else is in control of the engine."

The glider was tugged on a rope with a Y arrangement; there was a line on each wing that came together in front of the nose and ran on as a single line to the bomber doing the tugging. A telephone line ran along the rope, making possible voice communication between the pilot of the bomber and the glider pilot.

By midspring, Wallwork had qualified on Horsas, one of the first to do so. He was then shipped down to North Africa.

In March 1943, Rommel called von Luck to come see him at his headquarters near Benghazi. Von Luck drove up and together they dealt with some of the supply problems. Then Rommel asked von Luck to go for a walk. Rommel regarded von Luck as almost a second son, and he wanted to talk. "Listen," Rommel said, "one day you will remember what I am telling you. The war is lost."

Von Luck protested hotly. "We are very deep in Russia," he exclaimed. "We are in Scandinavia, in France, in the Balkans, in North Africa. How can the war be lost?"

"I will tell you," Rommel answered. "We lost Stalingrad, we will lose Africa, with the body of our best-trained armored people. We can't fight without them. The only thing we can do is to ask for an armistice. We have to give up all this business about the Jews, we have to change our minds about the religions, and so on, and we must get an armistice now at this stage while we still have something to offer."

Rommel asked von Luck to fly to Hitler's headquarters and plead with the Führer to execute a Dunkirk in reverse. It was all up in North Africa for the Axis, Rommel said, and he wanted to save his Afrika Korps. Von Luck went, but did not get past Field Marshal Jodl, who told von Luck that the Führer was in political discussions with the Rumanians and nobody wanted to butt in with military decisions. "And anyway," Jodl concluded, "there's no idea at all to withdraw from North

Africa." Von Luck never returned to Tunisia. Rommel flew out. The Afrika Korps was destroyed or captured.

Von Luck went on to teach at the military academy for half a year. In the late fall of 1943 he got orders to join the 21st Panzer Division in Brittany as one of the two regimental commanders. He had been specially requested by the division commander, Brigadier General Edgar Feuchtinger, who was close to Hitler and thus got the officers he wanted. Feuchtinger was reviving 21st Panzer from the dead, but his contact with Hitler made it a feasible task. His officers were exclusively veterans, most from Africa or the Eastern Front. The troops—almost sixteen thousand of them, as this was a full-strength division—were volunteers, young, eager, fit. The equipment was excellent, the tanks especially so. In addition, the new 21st Panzer had an abundance of SPVs (self-propelled vehicles), put together by a Major Becker, a reserve officer who was a genius with transport. He could transform any type of chassis into an SPV. On the SPVs he would mount all sorts of guns, but his favorite was the multibarreled rocket launcher, the so-called Stalin organ, with forty-eight barrels.

Von Luck set to with his regiment. Among many other exercises, he began to give the men extended night-training drills. At the end of 1943, Rommel—as commander of Army Group B—took control of the German Seventh Army in Normandy and Brittany. His arrival and his personality injected badly needed enthusiasm and professional skill into the building of the Atlantic Wall to protect Hitler's Fortress Europe.

Even Major Schmidt, guarding the bridges over the Orne waterways, caught some of the enthusiasm. He had come to Normandy some months earlier and quickly adjusted from frantic Nazi to a garrison soldier ready to enjoy the slow pace of the Norman countryside. He had put his men to work digging bunkers and slit trenches, and even an open machine-gun pit; with Rommel's arrival, the pace of construction sped up, and the scope of the defensive emplacements was greatly increased.

In March 1944, two reinforcements arrived at the bridge. One was Vern Bonck, who had got caught by the Gestapo in Warsaw, sent to a six-week training camp, where he could hardly understand the German NCOs, and then was posted to the 716th Infantry Division on the coast north of Caen. Helmut Romer had finished his Berlin schooling, been drafted, sent to training camp, and then was also posted to the 716th.

At the café, Thérèsa Gondrée had given birth to another daughter, to go with six-year-old Georgette.

Heinz Hickman spent most of 1943 fighting. He participated in the campaign in Sicily, then fought at Salerno and Cassino. At Cassino his regiment took such heavy losses that it had to be pulled back to Bologna for rebuilding and for training recruits. Through the winter of 1943–44, Hickman and his parachute regiment, like Howard and D Company, like von Luck and 21st Panzer, were training, training, training.

In June, Jim Wallwork went to Algeria, where he learned to fly Waco gliders, American-built gliders that landed on skids, carried only thirteen men, were difficult to handle, and were altogether despised by the British Glider Pilot Regiment. The pilots were delighted when they heard that Oliver Boland and some others were going to fly a few Horsas down to North Africa, all the way from England. Wallwork told his American instructors, "You, you be here tomorrow, you've got to be here to see a proper bloody glider. You'll really see something."

Then, "By golly, here came the first Halifax and Horsa combination." Turning to his instructor, Wallwork bellowed, "Look at that, you bloody Yank, there's a proper airplane, a proper glider, that's a proper thing. Oh, the truth of it!"

The Horsa cast off, did a circuit, came down, "and broke its bloody nose off. Imagine this. It was the first one in. Well, our American friends were delighted about that."

On the day of the invasion of Sicily, Jim flew a Waco with a lieutenant, ten riflemen, and a hand trailer full of ammunition. The tug pilots were Americans, flying Dakotas, which had no self-sealing tanks and no armored plate. Their orders were to avoid flak at all costs. When they approached the coastline and flak began to appear, most of the American pilots cast off their gliders and turned back to sea. As a consequence of being let go too far out, twenty of the twenty-four gliders never made it to shore. Many of the men were drowned (upon hearing this news, John Howard stepped up his swimming requirements).

In Jim's case, he kept telling the Dakota pilot, "Get in, get in." But the pilot would not get in; instead he turned away to sea. He made a second run and told Jim to drop off, but Jim would not; he could see that the coast was too far away, and he yelled, "Get in, get in." A third try, a third refusal by Jim to be let go. On the fourth pass, the Dakota pilot said calmly but firmly, "James, I'm going now. You've got to let go." Jim let go, thinking he could just make it. He did, skidding in over the beach, onto a little rough field, fairly close to an Italian machine-gun nest.

The Italians opened fire, "and we all jumped out; we knew by then to get out of the glider quickly." Jim turned his Sten gun on the Italians, thinking to himself, "Right, this will do you buggers." He pulled the trigger and nothing happened. The Sten had misfired. Fortunately the Bren gun knocked out the opposition. As the section then began to unload the glider, the lieutenant asked Wallwork, "Well, where in the hell are we? Do you know where we are?"

"As a matter of fact, sir," Jim replied, "I think you should be congratulated."

"Whatever for?"

"I think you are the first Allied officer to attack the soft underbelly of Europe through the toe of Italy."

Wallwork claims today that he was so confused by all the passes he had made at the beach that he really did think he had come down on the Continent proper. But his lieutenant merely snorted, "Well, I don't think much of that idea," and went about his tasks. Later that fall, Wallwork was shipped back to England to participate in operation Deadstick.

Deadstick was the result of decisions General Gale had made. Studying his tactical problem, Gale had decided that the best way to provide protection for the left flank of Sword Beach would be to blow up the bridges over the River Dives, through paratrooper assaults, then gather his paras in a semicircle around the bridges at Ranville and Bénouville, the ones that crossed the Orne waterway. Without those bridges, the Germans could not get at the left flank of the invasion. Gale could not afford to simply blow up the Orne bridges, however, because without them he would have an entire airborne division in the middle of enemy territory, its back to a major water barrier, without proper antitank weapons or other crucial supplies, and with no means of getting them.

The bridges had to be taken intact. Gale knew that they had a garrison guarding them, and that they had been prepared for demolition. Paras might be able to take the bridges, and certainly could destroy them, but would probably not be able to capture them intact. The relative slowness with which a para attack could be launched would give the Germans adequate time to blow the bridges themselves. Gale concluded that his only option was to seize the bridges by a coup de main, using Horsas, which could set twenty-eight fighting men beside a bridge simultaneously. Best of all, in gliders they could arrive like thieves in the night, without noise or light, unseen and unheard. Gale reports in his memoirs that he got the idea of a coup de main by studying German glider landings at Fort Eben Emael in Belgium in 1940 and the Corinth Canal in Greece in 1941. Gale was sure that if his glider pilots and his company commander were good enough, it could be done. He thought the real problem would be holding the bridges against counterattack until help could arrive from the paratroopers.

Gale briefed Brigadier Poett, explaining his conclusions and his reasoning. He told Poett he was putting the glider company under his, Poett's, command for the operation, because Poett's would be the para brigade that got to the gliders first. He told Poett, "The seizing of the bridges intact is of the utmost importance to the conduct of future operations. As the bridges will have been prepared for demolition, the speedy over-powering of the bridge defenses will be your first objective and it is therefore to be seized by the coup de main party. You must accept risks to achieve this."

Next Gale went to Kindersley, explained his coup de main idea, and asked Kindersley who was the best company commander in his brigade to carry out the mission. Kindersley replied, "I think that all my men are jolly good leaders, but I think Johnny Howard might do this one rather well." They decided to find out if he could.

Gale laid on a major three-day exercise. D Company was assigned to capture intact three small bridges and defend them until relieved. It was a night assault, with much of the division landing all over the area. The glider troops rode in trucks to prang. Umpires, riding in trucks, told them when they had landed. There were four gliderloads. They pranged at 2300 hours and after a brief struggle with the paras guarding the bridges, D Company managed to capture the structures before they were blown. "We had a really first-class fight," Howard recalls, despite the blank ammunition. Windy Gale and Hugh Kindersley and Nigel Poett were all there, watching.

At the debriefing, on April 18, Gale praised the "bridge prangers," as he called D Company, singling out for special citation the company's "dash and verve." That was highly pleasing for Howard and his men, of course, but what came next was even better. Colonel Mike Roberts called Howard into his office and began to bring him into the larger picture. Roberts said D Company would have a "very important task to carry out when the invasion started. You are to capture two bridges, intact. The bridges are about a quarter of a mile apart and each is fifty yards long."

Looking up, Roberts stared at Howard, then said, "You will be the spearhead of the invasion, certainly the first British fighting force to land on the Continent." Usually a nondemonstrative man who spent most of his time worrying, Roberts was deeply moved. He told Howard it was a great, great honor for the Ox and Bucks to provide the company for such a task.

Roberts warned Howard that all the information was Top Secret, and said he had been brought in only because Gale was laying on another, even larger exercise, code name Mush, which would in fact be a rehearsal for D-Day. Howard should approach the exercise with that in mind. Further, Gale had decided, on the basis of the previous exercise, to strengthen D Company from four to six platoons. Roberts told Howard to select any two platoons he wanted from the regiment.

Howard selected two platoons from B Company, one commanded by Sandy Smith, the other by Dennis Fox. Both lieutenants were keen athletes, perfectly fit, boyishly enthusiastic about their sports, former Cambridge students who were popular with their men. Howard told Brian Priday to extend the invitation; Priday pulled Smith and Fox out of their quarters one evening "and said to us in great secrecy, 'Would you like to join our little party which we're going to do and we can't tell you much more than that but are you prepared to join D Company?'"

Smith and Fox looked at each other. They both thought the Army a bit of a bore, and they especially disliked regular soldiers, and most of all they hated the fanatics. John Howard was the leading fanatic in the regiment. Furthermore, Fox and Smith enjoyed "chasing women and having a good time. We were very high spirited and that bunch of D Company officers, they used to bore the living daylights out of us. Sweeney, Brotheridge, Hooper, Priday, Wood—that whole bunch of fanatics—we didn't want to get near them. And come to that, they thought us very peculiar." But to pass up a Top Secret special mission was unthinkable, and Smith and Fox joined up. To their surprise, they merged with D Company immediately and without difficulty.

D Company was further reinforced by the addition of thirty sappers under Captain Jock Neilson. The sappers were Royal Engineers, but also paratroopers. Howard recalled that when they reported to him, "those paraboys were quite definite about not landing in gliders." Howard explains, "There is a good healthy respect between the paraboys and the gliderboys, but I can't resist saying that whereas a high percentage of us would willingly jump out of a plane on a chute into battle, you would have to go a long way to get a glider-load of paraboys to prang into battle in a Horsa."

Before Mush was held, D Company got a two-week leave. Joy had by then bought a small house in Oxford, where John went to see his newborn daughter, Penny, for the first time. It was on this occasion that John left his dress uniform behind, and took Terry's baby shoe with him. Laughing, Joy relates that back in 1940, when fear of an invasion was high, John had left her with a Luger pistol, after instructing her in its use. In April 1944, when he left, she noticed that he had taken the bullets with him. She assumed he was afraid that he might not come back and she would kill herself out of love for him. Laughing again, Joy says she couldn't even lift the pistol, much less use it.

Den Brotheridge too had a visit with his wife of one year, Margaret, who was seven months pregnant. Wally Parr was with Irene in London's East End. Most of the other chaps managed to visit their families.

At the end of April, everyone reported back to Bulford, all leaves were canceled until further notice, and operation Mush was held. D Company was to attack, capture, and hold a bridge until relieved by the paras. All six platoons and the sappers participated. They were driven to the site of the maneuver, then marched a couple of miles through the night to their supposed LZ, then told by the umpire with them to lie down and wait for his signal telling them they had pranged. They were only a few hundred yards from the bridge, which was being guarded by Polish paratroopers.

With the signal from the umpire, D Company began to move forward silently. Tony Hooper was first through the barbed wire, and with his platoon rushed the bridge. The umpires declared the bridge had been blown. Howard recalls, "I saw Tony on the bridge arguing heatedly with an irate umpire who had put him out of action together with most of his platoon. The umpire won and the men sat disconsolate on the bridge with their helmets off."

The umpires declared that Sweeney's platoon also had been put out of action, by fire from Brotheridge's platoon. Sweeney had not recognized Brotheridge's men as together they crept silently toward the bridge. Howard learned a lesson from the experience.

Mush was a well conceived and conducted rehearsal. The exercise revealed problems, in short, such as mutual recognition in the dark, but it also convinced Howard, and his many superiors who watched, that if the Horsas pranged on the right spot, the coup de main would work.

The sine qua non, of course, was getting the Horsas down where they belonged. To that end, Jim Wallwork and the Glider Pilot Regiment were working day and night, literally, on operation Deadstick. In April 1944, Wallwork and his fellow pilots had done a demonstration for Gale, operation Skylark, landing their Horsas on a small triangle from six thousand feet. When all the gliders were safely down, the GPR commanding officer, Colonel George Chatteron, stepped out of the bushes. He had General Gale with him. Chatteron was boasting, "Well, Windy, there you see it, I told you my GPR boys can do this kind of thing any day." Wallwork overheard the remark and thought, "I wish we could, but that is a bit of asking."

To make sure they could, Gale put them on operation Deadstick. Sixteen pilots of the GPR, two for each of the six gliders going in on D-Day plus four backups, were posted to Tarrent Rushton, a major airfield where there were two Halifax squadrons and a squadron of Horsas. The men of the GPR were treated as very special people indeed. They had their own Nissen hut, excellent food, a captain delegated to them—they were all sergeants—to see to it that their every want was catered to. As Oliver Boland recalled it, "We were the most pampered . . . group of people in the British Army at the time."

The pilots were introduced to their tug crews. This was an innovation; previously the glider pilots had not known their tug pilots. The tug crews lived near the GPR boys at Tarrent Rushton, and they got to know one another. The glider pilots had the same crew on each training flight, the crew that would tug them on D-Day.

The training flights for operation Deadstick were hellishly difficult. Colonel Chatteron had the pilots landing beside a small L-shaped wood, a quarter of a mile long down the long end, and a few yards along the angle. The pilots landed with three gliders going up the L and three on the blind side, carrying cement blocks for a load. In daylight, on a straight-in run, it was a snap. But next Chatteron started having them release at seven thousand feet, then fly by times and courses, using a stopwatch, making two or three full turns before coming in over the wood. That was not too bad either, because—as Wallwork explains—"in broad daylight you can always cheat a little." Next Chatteron put colored glass in their flying goggles, which turned day into night, and warned his pilots, "It is silly of you to cheat on this because you've got to do it right when the time comes." Wallwork would nevertheless whip the goggles off if he thought he was overshooting. "But we began to play it fairly square, realizing that whatever we were going to do it was going to be something important."

By early May, they were flying by moonlight, casting off at six thousand feet, seven miles from the wood. They flew regardless of weather. They twisted and turned in the sky, all by stopwatch. They did forty-three training flights in Deadstick altogether, more than half of them at night. They got ready.

4

D-DAY MINUS ONE MONTH TO D-DAY

ON MAY 2, Howard was summoned to Broadmore, code name for Gale's planning headquarters, an old country place full of rickety stairs and low beams, near Milston on Salisbury Plain. It was surrounded by barbed wire and had elaborate security precautions. Once inside, Howard was taken to Brigadier Poett's office. Poett explained that D Company was being detached from the Ox and Bucks and given a special assignment, then handed Howard his orders, marked "Bigot" and "Top Secret," dated May 2, and signed by Poett. The orders were "to seize *intact* the bridges over the River Orne and canal at Bénouville and Ranville, and to hold them until relief."

The orders contained information on enemy dispositions that Howard could expect to encounter. "The garrison of the two bridges consists of about 50 men," the orders read, armed with four to six light machine guns, one or two antitank guns of less than 50-mm caliber, and a heavy machine gun. "A concrete shelter is under construction, and the bridges will have been prepared for demolition." There was a battalion of the 736th Grenadier Regiment in the area, with eight to twelve tanks under command, and with motor transport. At least one company would be standing to as a fighting patrol, ready to move out at once to seek information. Howard should expect the enemy to be "in a high state of alertness. The bridge garrison may be standing to, and charges will have been laid in the demolition chambers."

At this point in his reading Howard may have wondered how on earth General Gale expected him to seize intact bridges that were prepared for demolition. All the enemy had to do was press a button or move a switch and up would go the bridges. Gale himself, in his 1948 book, *The 6th Airborne Division in Normandy*, explains his thinking about this problem: "There is always or nearly always a slip between the cup and the lip: orders are vague: there is uncertainty: has the moment arrived or should one wait? Who is the individual actually responsible both for working the switch and for ordering the bridges to be blown? These questions are age-old and on the doubts that might exist in some German mind or minds at the critical moment I based the plan. But a moment or two was all that I knew we would get. The assault on the bridges must, therefore, come like a bolt from the blue."

Howard's orders of May 2 informed him that his initial relief would come from the 5th Para Brigade, which would drop northeast of Ranville at 0050 hours and then "move forthwith to take up a defensive position round the two bridges." Simultaneously, 3d Para Brigade would drop on the high wooded ground south of Le Mesnil forest. At 0600, the British 3d Infantry Division would begin its landings west of Ouistreham "with objective Caen."

Attached to the 3d Division were Lord Lovat's Commandos, who would move forward as rapidly as possible to establish a land link between the beaches and the paratroopers and gliderborne troops in and around the bridges. The brigade of Commandos could be expected any time after 1100 hours.

To carry out his assignment, Howard was given his own D Company, plus two platoons from B Company, a detachment of thirty sappers, one wing of the Glider Pilot Regiment, and six Horsa gliders. Poett's May 2 orders also gave Howard the general outline of how he should proceed.

"The capture of the bridges will be a coup de main operation depending largely on surprise, speed and dash for success," the orders read. "Provided the bulk of your force lands safely, you should have little difficulty in overcoming the known opposition on the bridges. Your difficulties will arise in holding off an enemy counterattack on the bridges, until you are relieved."

Turning specifically to the subject of counterattack, Poett's orders continued, "You must expect a counterattack any time after" 0100 hours, or within an hour of landing. "This attack may take the form of a battle group consisting of one company infantry in lorries, up to eight tanks and one or two guns mounted on lorries, or it may be a lorried infantry company alone, or infantry on foot." The most likely line of approach for the counterattacking force would be from the west.

Howard was ordered to organize his defensive position immediately after taking the bridges, because "it is vital that the crossing places be held, and to do this you will secure a close bridgehead on the west bank, in addition to guarding the bridges. The immediate defense of the bridges and of the west bank of the canal must be held at all costs." Poett's orders envisioned more than a passive defense, however. "You will harass and delay the deployment of the enemy counterattack forces . . . by offensive patrols," the orders read. "Patrols will remain mobile and offensive. Up to one-third of your effective force may be used in this role. The remaining two-thirds will be used for static defense and immediate counterattack."

Poett was also explicit in the orders as to the role of the sappers. He told Howard to give them "the following tasks only, in order of priority: neutralizing the demolition mechanisms, removing charges from demolition chambers, and establishing ferries." He also promised that one company of the 7th Para Battalion of the 5th Para Brigade would "be dispatched to your assistance with the utmost possible speed after the landing of the brigade. They should reach your position by 0230 hours, and will come under your command until arrival of the officer commanding 7th Para Battalion."

Poett concluded his orders: "The training of your force will be regarded as a first priority matter." He encouraged Howard to make "demands for special stores and training facilities," and promised to "give you every possible help."

When Howard finished reading the orders, Poett told him verbally that he did not intend to interfere with D

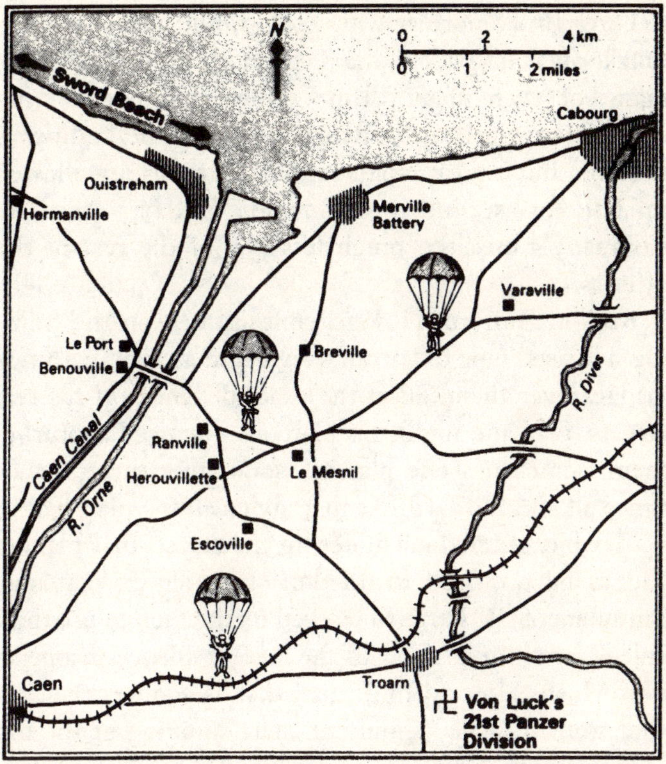

Company's preparation for the coup de main. Howard would have the twin responsibilities of designing an effective training program and of making the detailed plan for the seizure of the bridges.

Howard could scarcely keep his feelings to himself. He was concerned about the various challenges he faced, of course, and could imagine any number of things going wrong. But he was also exhilarated, as he had never been before in his life, and tremendously proud that D Company had been chosen to lead the way on D-Day.

Poett gave Howard a green pass, which allowed him

to enter Broadmore at will. Poett would not allow him to take away his orders, the reconnaissance photographs, maps, or even notes. "But," Howard remarks, "that didn't stop me from thinking. Being in the know was exciting, but a great mental strain." He was not allowed to tell his second-in-command, Priday, about D Company's mission, much less any of the rest of the officers.

Back at Bulford, Howard concentrated on the training. He used tape to lay out a river and a canal, with two bridges over them, all at the exact distances of his real targets. Day and night, his platoons practiced capturing them; sometimes one platoon, sometimes three, sometimes all six. Howard felt that above all his plan had to be flexible. If only one glider hit the target, that platoon had to be prepared to do the job of all six platoons. Simultaneously, Howard worked on the men to use their voices, reminding them of the cost of silence in operation Mush. Howard told them that as soon as the first shot went off, they should all start shouting at the top of their lungs. Number 1 glider was Able, #2 was Baker, #3 was Charley, and so on. Howard wanted the men to shout out their identifications, over and over, both to identify one another and to give the Germans the feeling that the enemy was there in great numbers.

From these exercises over the taped bridges and roads, Howard decided that General Gale's plan for landing inside, that is between the bridges, rather than outside them, was correct. The LZs on the inside were awfully small, to be sure, and so situated that one group of gliders, at the canal bridge, would have to land facing north, toward the coast, the other group facing south, toward Caen, which required splitting the glider formations at takeoff. These disadvantages were outweighed by two major advantages: the inside landing sites were smack against the bridges, instead of some distance away; and by having all his platoons inside, Howard could call on them to support one another.

Broadmore, meanwhile, was making its intelligence on the bridges and surrounding villages available to Howard. Thanks to Georges Gondrée and Mme. Vion, the Resistance in Caen, and the photo reconnaissance of the RAF, there was a rather fabulous amount available. Division intelligence was able to tell Howard who were the collaborators in Bénouville, who were Resistance. He knew that Georges Gondrée understood English, his wife, German. He was given a complete topographical report on the area. He knew that Bénouville contained 589 residents, that M. Thomas was the mayor, that the voltage was 110/200 three-phase AC. He was warned that from the roof of the Château de Bénouville, a three-story building that was a maternity hospital with fifteen beds and twelve reception rooms, the Germans would have a commanding field of fire over the valley of the Orne River for a considerable distance.

Howard was also told that Mme. Vion, the director of the hospital, was head of the Resistance. Mme. Vion, he was told, "was quite an autocratic sort of person and considered to be the lady of the village, as we would call her in this country." He even knew that many in the village looked sideways when Thérèsa Gondrée walked past, because they were suspicious of her German accent and because she was living right next to the garrison, selling beer to the Germans.

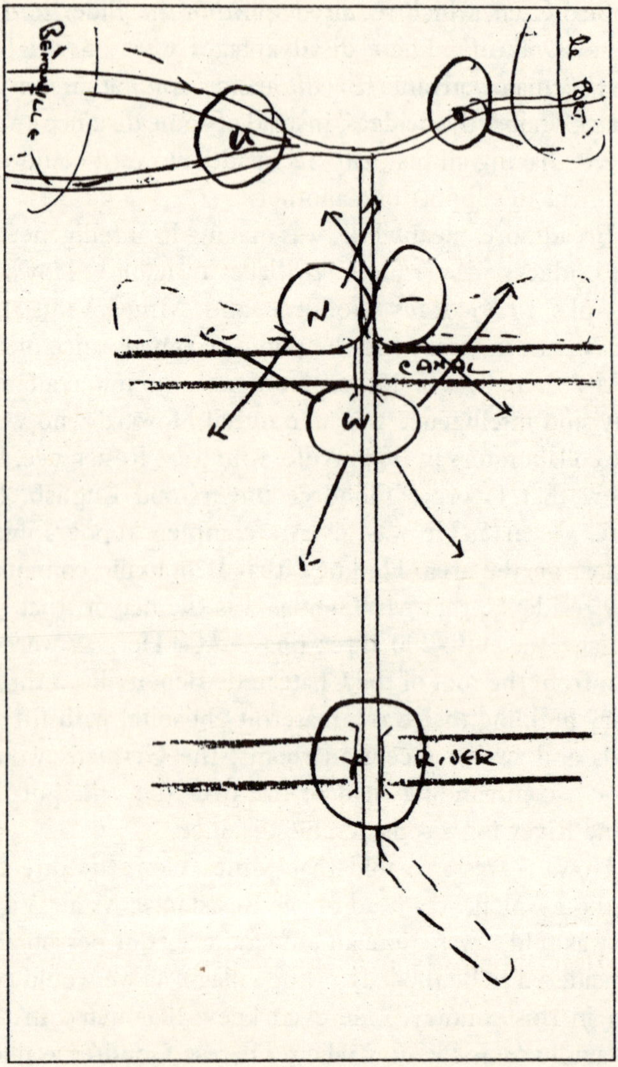

Sketch made by John Howard early in the planning for the Pegasus operation showing the planned disposition of the platoons if all landed on target.

Below: A topographical report on the bridges dated 17 May 1944. The superb quality of the information provided by both the French Resistance and reconnaissance aircraft is shown clearly.

NEPTUNE
BIGOT—TOP SECRET

Copy No......./..

17 May 44

TOPOGRAPHICAL REPORT ON BRIDGES AT BENOUVILLE 098748 AND RANVILLE 104746

1. **Sketch—BENOUVILLE 098748**

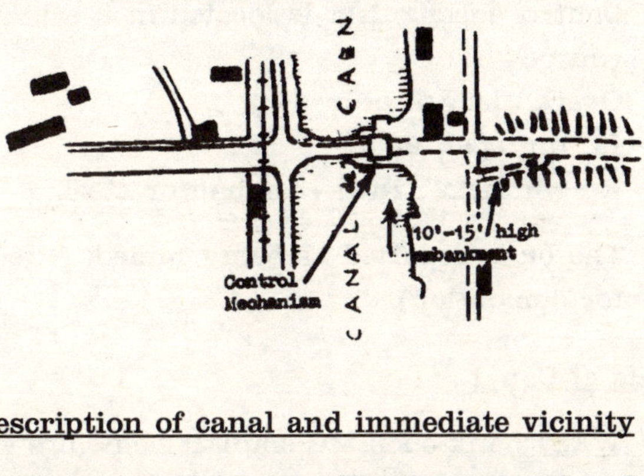

2. **Description of canal and immediate vicinity**

(a) The current is slow. Depth reported to be 27' but can be regulated by the locks at OUISTREHAM. Average width 150'. Banks average 6' in height, and are of earth and broken stone.

(b) A track with waterbound macadam surface

runs for most of the length of the canal on both sides. On the WEST bank there is a lt rly (single track). Either bank of the canal is lined with poplars. On each side of the br there are a few small houses. (For detail see large scale model).

(c) The rd leading up to the br is on a 10'–15' high embankment to keep it above the flood level.

3. <u>Description of Br</u>

(a) The water gap is 190' but from either bank there are abutments which project 50' into the stream.

(b) The br is a steel girder, rolling lift br with masonry abutments.
Control mechanism is located in a cabin <u>over</u> rdway.
Overall length of br 190'
Lifting span 90'
Rd width 12', rdway asphalt or steel.

(c) The br is reported as being mined. (Prepared for demolition).

4. <u>Defs of Canal</u>

(a) <u>WEST bank</u> open MG emplacements are visible on the canal banks on each side of the br approach. There are further open MG emplacements at 098748(2), 097748(2) and 096746.

(b) <u>EAST side.</u> SOUTH of rd close to the canal bank is a circular emplacement approx 27' in diameter which is probable site for an atk gun but the object in the emplacement cannot be identified as a gun. 25 yds SOUTH of the above is an AA MG post on a tower 8' high.

(c) 60 yds NORTH of the rd close to the canal are 3 open MG emplacements, 12 yds apart, in a line facing NE.
Approx 16 yds NE of these emplacements is a concrete shelter or pillbox, measuring approx 17' x 14'.

(d) No wire defs are visible.

(e) Armed trawlers and R Boats may be used in canal but this is considered unlikely.

. . . /5 . . .

5. <u>Description of R ORNE</u>

(a) Average width 160'–240'.
Tidal as far as CAEN.
Mean depth 9'
Max tidal variation at OUISTREHAM 16'.
" " " " CAEN 6' 5".
Banks 3' 6" high, of mud, and slope at approx 1:2.

(b) There is a barrage at CAEN which regulates the canal at the expense of the river, hence speed and depth will vary considerably. Max current will probably NOT exceed 3 Knots.

(c) Ground between the river and canal is marshy and intersected by many ditches and channels.

(d) A track 8'–10' wide runs on both sides of the river for most of its length.

6. Description of br 104745 and immediate vicinity.

(a) The br is a two-span, cantilever lattice girder, pivoted about a central masonry pier. Turning mechanism is housed over pier between girders.
Overall length of br 350'.
Spans, 2 at 100'.
Load class 12.
Rdway—9' tarmac (20' incl sidewalks).
It is thought that this br may no longer be used as a swing br.
Br has been reported as prepared for demolition.

(b) SOUTH of the rd and WEST of the river is an orchard running NORTH and SOUTH.
Each bank of the river is lined with poplars.
On the EAST of the river and SOUTH of the rd is a thick belt of trees running parallel to the river, and about 50 yds away.
Both NORTH and SOUTH of the rd there are a few small houses, standing in gardens or orchards. For details see large-scale model.

7. Defs on R ORNE

(a) EAST end and on the SOUTH side of the rd is a cam pill-box measuring approx 16' x 16'. This may contain an atk weapon with main line of fire EAST along rd.

There is a small AA MG emplacement adjoining this pill-box on the WEST side.

(b) EAST side. Two open MG emplacements are visible on the NORTH side of the rd.

(c) There is no wire visible.

(d) Two rd-blocks (probably tree trunks) lie alongside the rd at 105745 and 106744.

Maj

APO ENGLAND **BM 6 Airldg Bde**

DL

Howard also knew that the garrison at the bridge was part of the 736th Grenadier Regiment of the 716th Infantry Division. On his intelligence summary, stamped "Bigot," he read that "the fighting value of this division has been assessed at 40% static and 15% in a counterattack role. Equipment consists of an unknown proportion of French, British, and Polish weapons." The last sentence read, "This intelligence summary will be destroyed by fire immediately after reading." (Howard saved it anyway.)

Howard could not take the air-reconnaissance photographs out of Broadmore, but he could go there to study them any time he wished. The RAF people had set up a stereograph system for him, which gave him a three-dimensional view. As Gale and Poett went over the photographs with Howard, they kept telling him that he had to capture those bridges in a few minutes, before they could be blown. The role, even the survival, of the

6th Airborne Division depended on having possession of those bridges, intact.

How good, and how up to date, was Howard's intelligence? As good as it could possibly be. Of all the attributes the British people demonstrated during World War II, none equaled their ability to gather, evaluate, and disseminate intelligence. Without question, they were the best in the world at it. The British government invested heavily in intelligence in all its various forms, and received a handsome return. John Howard was one of the beneficiaries. Here are three examples of what he got.

In early May, Rommel visited the bridges. He ordered an antitank gun emplacement built, and a pillbox to protect it, with barbed wire around it. He also ordered more slit trenches dug. The work began immediately. Within two days, Howard was told by the RAF that Jerry was installing some suspicious emplacements. Within a week, word came via Gondrée through Vion to Caen to British intelligence to Broadmore to Howard that the gun emplacement had an antitank gun in it, with some camouflage over it, and that the pillbox was finished.

In mid-May, 21st Panzer Division moved from Britany to Normandy, and on May 23 to the Caen area, with von Luck's regiment taking up positions just east of Caen. On May 24, Howard knew about the movement of the division. On May 25, Hickman's Independent Parachute Regiment moved into the area; Howard knew about it the next day.

The intelligence people produced a model of the area, twelve feet by twelve feet. Howard describes it as "indeed a work of art, every building, tree, bush and ditch, trench, fence, etc., was there." The model was changed daily, in accordance with the results of that morning's reconnaissance flight. Thus on May 15 Schmidt knocked down two buildings along the canal, to give him a better field of fire, and Howard saw the change on the model the next day.

Howard's visits to Broadmore were characterized by the place's nickname, "The Madhouse." After clearing numerous checkpoints with his green pass, Howard recalls going in and being struck by "the harassed look on the faces of people walking about the building, obviously up to their eyes in last-minute changes in major plans."

At the end of his early-May briefing, Poett had told Howard, "Anything you want, John, it's there. You've only gotta ring up for it." Howard ordered up German opposition for his exercises—that is, the bridge defenders wore German uniforms, used German weapons and tactics, and insofar as possible shouted out their orders in German. He got captured German rifles, carbines, and machine guns, German mortars, German hand grenades, so that all his men were thoroughly familiar with what these weapons could do, and how to operate them. He had but to snap his fingers, and trucks would appear, to carry his platoons to wherever he wanted to go.

D Company got the best of everything, except in food, in which area it got no special favors. The food was bad; worse, there was not enough of it. Parr recalls, "Much of your money, spare money, went on grub. I was always hungry. You worked so hard, you trained so hard that the grub they gave you wasn't enough to keep you going and you didn't ask what it was, you just grabbed it and you just shoveled it down, as simple as that. So the first thing you got paid you used to make out for the NAAFI and get chow. Yeah, you supplemented your diet with your pay, there's no doubt about that."

Howard was pushing the men hard now, harder than ever, but no matter how he varied the order of landing or direction of attack or other aspects of the exercise, they were always the same make-believe bridges, at the same distances. Everyone was getting bored stiff. After about ten days of this, Howard called the men together on the parade ground and told them, "Look, we are training for some special purpose." He did not mention the invasion—he hardly had to—but he went on: "You'll find that a lot of the training we are doing, this capturing of things like bridges, is connected with that special purpose. If any of you mention the word 'bridges' outside our training hours and I get to know about it, you'll be for the high jump and your feet won't touch before you are RTU." (Wally Parr told Irene the next evening, over the telephone, that he would be doing bridges on D-Day.)

Von Luck, as noted, had moved to the east of Caen, between the River Dives and the Orne River. So had Hickman. Von Luck planned, and practiced, his defenses. He marked out the routes forward to alternative assembly areas behind likely invasion points. He laid down rest and refueling areas, detailed traffic-control units, marked bypasses, and allotted antiaircraft guns for road protection. Hickman meanwhile was engaging in antiparatrooper exercises. Even Major Schmidt, at the bridges, was getting some sense of urgency. He was completing his bunkers, and was almost ready to get around to putting in the antiglider poles.

The Gondrées watched all this, and said nothing, except to Mme. Vion.

Howard asked the topographical people to search the map of Britain and find him some place where a river and a canal ran closely together and were crossed by bridges on the same road. They found such a spot outside Exeter. Howard moved the company down there, and for six days, by day and by night, attacked those Exeter bridges.

Townspeople came to gape as the lads dashed about, throwing grenades, setting off explosives, getting into hand-to-hand combat, cursing, yelling "Able, Able" or "Easy, Easy" at the top of their lungs. Howard had them practice every possible development he could imagine—only one glider getting down, or the gliders landing out of the proper sequence, or the dozens of other possibilities. He taught every man the basic rudiments of the sappers' jobs; he instructed thc sappers in the functions of the platoons; he made certain that each of his officers was prepared to take command of the whole operation, if need be.

Howard insisted that they all become proficient in putting together and using the canvas boats that he was bringing along in the event the bridges were blown. Assault-boat training was "always good for morale," according to Howard, because "somebody inevitably went overboard and that poor individual never failed to make sure he wasn't the only one who got wet."

The hurling about of grenades caused some problems and brought some fun. Grenades were tossed into the river, to provide fish for supper. The Town Council protested this illegal fishing. The Council also protested that all this running back and forth over its bridges and all these grenades going off were seriously weakening the structures. (They stand, solid, today.) A homeowner in the area had some tiles blown off his roof by a grenade. Irate, he confronted Howard, who passed him along to Priday, who gave him the proper forms to fill in so that he could get the tiles replaced. One month later, sitting in a foxhole in Normandy, Priday let out a whoop of laughter. The mail had been delivered, and in it was a letter from the homeowner to Priday, demanding to know when his roof would be fixed.

Out of all this practice, Howard made his final plan. The key to it was to put the pillbox out of action while simultaneously getting a platoon across the bridge and onto that side of the road. It had to be accomplished before shots were fired, if possible, and certainly before the Germans were fully aroused. The pillbox was a key not only because of its firing power, but because that was where the button that could blow the bridge was located. Howard detailed three men from #1 glider (Brotheridge's platoon) to dash to the pillbox and throw grenades through the slits. To take physical possession of the opposite bank, Howard detailed Brotheridge to lead the remainder of his platoon on a dash across the bridge. Ideally, Howard wanted Brotheridge to hear the thuds of the grenades in the pillbox as he was midway across the bridge.

Number 2 glider, David Wood's platoon, would clear up the inner defenses, the trenches and machine-gun nests along the east bank. Number 3 glider, Sandy

Smith's platoon, would cross the bridge to reinforce Brotheridge. On the river bridge, the procedure would be the same, with Priday in #4 glider (Hooper's platoon), Fox in #5, and Sweeney in #6.

Each glider would carry five of the thirty men under the command of Captain R. K. Jock Neilson. The sappers' job was to move immediately to the bridges, then hand-over-hand themselves along the bottom beams, cutting fuses and looking for and disposing of explosives.

It was John Howard's plan. His superiors let him work it out himself, then approved his final presentation. He ran through it again and again, until the men were exhausted and both too tense and too bored to care any longer.

But each time he ran through it, Howard saw something he had overlooked. One day, for example, he stopped an exercise and said he had been thinking that if so and so happened, and such and such, he'd need volunteers to swim the canal with a Bren gun to set up a flanking fire. As Howard remembers the occasion, "competition for this hazardous mission was high." As Parr remembers it, he raised his hand before Howard could call for volunteers. Howard impatiently told him to put it down. Parr waved it some more.

"Oh, all right, Parr, what is it?"

"Well, sir," Parr replied, "it's just this: as Billy Gray and Charlie Gardner here are our two strongest swimmers, why not detail them?"

"Excellent idea, Parr," Howard pronounced, and it was done. Parr spent the remainder of the week staying far away from Gray and Gardner.

* * *

The last night in Exeter was a classic eve-of-battle event. Howard gave the men the night off, they poured into and out of Exeter's pubs, there were fights, windows were broken. The chief of police got Howard on the phone; Howard and Priday jumped into a jeep and tore into Exeter, about three miles away, "and as we crossed the bridge we were picked up by the police for speeding, and we arrived at the station with police escort." Howard strode into the chief's office and said, "If you find Lieutenant Brotheridge he will put you in charge with how to get the troops back." Then Howard looked around and saw the chief's World War I medals, "and I knew the type of chap I was talking to, and I explained to this chap in very few words that this was our last night out, and his attitude was absolutely wonderful." The chief called out the entire force and put it to rounding up D Company and escorting it gently back to its encampment.

Brotheridge, in fact, turned out to be no help, although Howard had sent him along with the men specifically to exert a calming influence. But he was too much like the men to stay sober on a night like this. Besides, he had a lot on his mind, and he needed some mental relief. His baby was due in less than a month, but he could not expect to see his wife before then, and who could tell about afterward? He was proud that Howard had chosen him to lead #1 platoon, but he had to be realistic—everyone knew that the first man over that bridge was the man most likely to get shot. Not killed, necessarily, but almost certainly shot. That first man was equally likely to have the bridge blow in his face.

To escape such thoughts, Brotheridge had gone

drinking with his sergeants, and when Howard arrived, Brotheridge was hopelessly drunk. Howard drove him back to camp, while the trucks took the men home. The people of Exeter and their police chief never made a complaint.

In late May, D Company moved to Tarrent Rushton. On this huge base, completely secured, no one in or out without a pass, the company met Jim Wallwork and John Ainsworth and Oliver Boland and the other pilots. Howard was pleased to note that they were absorbed into the company as family members as quickly as the sappers had been.

How dependent D Company was on the pilots became quickly apparent after arrival in Tarrent Rushton. Now that the company was properly sealed in, Howard was free to give his briefing. First to the officers, then to the men, he explained the coup de main operation.

Howard covered the walls of the Nissen briefing hut with aerial photographs of the bridges. He had the model in the middle of the room. As he talked, the eyes of the officers and men opened wider and wider—at the amount of intelligence available to them, at the crucial nature of their task, and at the idea of being the first men to touch the soil of France. But what they also noted was the extreme smallness of the LZs, especially on the canal bridge. Having examined the German trench system, and discussed the weapons and emplacements the Germans had, the officers—and later the men—were completely confident that they could take the bridges intact. They could, that is, if—and only if—the pilots put them down on the right spots.

* * *

The pilots were now into the last days of Deadstick. Calling on the British movie industry for help, the Air Ministry had put together a film. By flipping through thousands of photographs, each ever so slightly different, the producers made a "moving picture" that depicted the actual flight the pilots would make on D-Day. There was a running commentary.

"The viewer felt as if he were in the cockpit and flying the thing," Wallwork recalls. The commentary told altitude, airspeed, location. When the glider cast off, "You got the whole sensation of diving a thousand feet and seeing the fields of France coming up toward you." Level off, turn, turn again, then the bridges were in view. "You come into this fly-in," as Wallwork describes the film, "and you are still on this bearing and the next thing you saw was the tower of the bridge getting nearer and nearer and then the film cuts out as you crash." The pilots could see the film whenever they wanted, and they watched it often. "It was absolutely fantastic," Wallwork declares. "Invaluable."

Howard briefed the men over and over, by sections and by platoons. He encouraged them to go into the hut whenever they wished, examine the maps and the photographs and the model, and talk among themselves about their particular tasks.

On May 29, he called the reinforced company together and issued the escape aids. "Very Boy Scoutish things," Howard says, including a metal file to be sewed into the battle smock, a brass pants button that contained a tiny compass, a silk scarf with the map of France on it, water-purifying tablets, and French francs. "These sorts of things absolutely thrilled the troops to bits," Howard recalls. "I have never seen such enthusiasm about a simple thing like that." Billy Gray remembers that all the French money was gambled away in two hours.

That night, in Normandy, von Luck was conducting exercises designed to counter any landing, even commando, by an immediate counterattack. Von Luck recalls, "The idea was absolutely clear, if there would be any landing, you had to start immediately to counterattack to throw the enemy back into the sea."

That day, Major Schmidt received a shipment of slave laborers from the Todt Organization, and put them to work digging holes for antiglider poles, in what he figured were the most likely LZs for gliders. He began with the areas around his bridges. The poles themselves had not yet arrived, but were expected daily.

When, on May 30, Howard and all of D Company saw the photographic evidence of the holes, their first reaction was that somehow the great secret had escaped, that the Germans knew where they were coming. Kindersley came down to visit Howard, guessing correctly that Howard would be in a blue mood.

"I know about those photographs, John," he began, "but there is nothing to worry about." Howard voiced his fear: all those photographs taken by the RAF for the movie for the pilots, all those photographs each morning, surely the Germans must have figured out that because of all that reconnaissance activity D Company was coming to the bridges. Kindersley laughed. "John," he said, "we're taking similar photographs of every bridge or target between the Bay of Biscay and Dunkirk."

That relieved one worry. Howard went to Wallwork with the other worry. "Supposing the poles are put into the holes before we land? What will be our chances?"

"That's just what we want, sir," Wallwork answered.

"What do you mean? What can you mean?" Howard asked.

"Well, you know we are kinda overloaded into that field; it's very narrow and what makes things worse is right at the end, where the road is, there's an embankment. Well, if we hit that, you know, we are going out in a hell of a crash; this is the thing that is worrying me more than anything. Now, those poles will take something off one wing and something off the other wing—it's just damned cheap plywood, you know—and those poles will pull us up absolutely beautifully."

Howard's face brightened. "Right," he said, "Well, let's get the company on parade." He called the men together, let them mumble and rumble awhile, mostly about those holes, then explained to them what Kindersley had told him about photographing everywhere, not just their bridges. Next he asked Wallwork to tell the company what he had just said about the poles being exactly what was needed. Wallwork did so, and the men were satisfied.

"Put it down to ignorance," Wally Parr explains, "call it what you like, we could see the situation. But Johnny Howard said it could be done and Wallwork said we could do it and that was the end of the subject. If Johnny Howard said we could do it, we could do it."

Besides the poles, Wallwork had to worry about Howard's request that he break down the barbed wire with the nose of his Horsa, a difficult enough task with an unloaded glider in daylight on a runway. And his glider and all the others were grossly overloaded, with thirty or thirty-one men in each, plus ammunition. There were two assault boats per glider. The sappers had heavy equipment. The men were carrying up to twenty pounds more ammunition each than had been allotted, and still were trying to add more to their load.

Wallwork told Howard that the extra weight might make the Horsa unmanageable, and certainly would increase the airspeed, and thus landing speed, requiring a longer landing area than was available. Howard told Captain Neilson of the Royal Engineers to get rid of some weight by dropping off one sapper per glider, but Neilson convinced Howard that he absolutely had to have all his sappers. Howard removed one boat from each glider. Not enough, Wallwork told him. Six hundred more pounds per glider had to go.

Howard reluctantly made his decision. Two privates from each platoon would have to drop out. It was a "terrible decision," he recalls. He gave it to his platoon commanders and told them to select the men to be left behind. In Brotheridge's platoon, Billy Gray says, "We all started shouting, 'Parr's married, let Parr drop out. Let's get rid of Parr!' And Wally immediately did his nut, and he was allowed to stay."

The lieutenants made the choices. The next day, Howard says, "I had men asking to see me at company office and crying their eyes out; a big, tough, bloody airborne soldier crying his eyes out asking to be left on the team. It was a very touching moment, I tell you, to weed out those people at that time; it was an awful moment for them."

At one of his briefings, Howard had asked for questions. "Sir," someone piped up, "can't we have a doctor? We are going in on our own and all." Howard thought that an excellent idea, asked Poett if he could get a volunteer from the division medical staff, and Dr John Vaughan came to join D Company. That meant another private had to be bumped. Fortunately, a soldier in Smith's platoon sprained his ankle playing soccer.

Vaughan has a nice anecdote to illustrate Howard's exuberance in the last days before the invasion. On May 31, Vaughan and Howard drove to Broadmore, Howard driving much too fast, as he always did. When they arrived, who should be standing there as Howard screeched the brakes but Brigadier Poett. Howard jumped out of the jeep, leapt high in the air, came down directly in front of Poett, snapped to attention, gave a full and quite grand salute, and shouted, "Sir!"

That same night, Smith and Fox sneaked out of Tarrent Rushton (neither of them can recall how they managed it) to have dinner in a local hotel with their girl friends (both remember the meal and the girls vividly).

That evening, Wallwork and the other pilots were given a special set of orders. These said that the bearer was not responsible to anyone, that he was to be returned to the U.K. by the most expeditious means, and that this order overruled all other orders. It was signed "Bernard Law Montgomery." Poett also told Howard privately, "Whatever you do, John, don't let those pilots get into combat. They are much too valuable to be wasted. Get them back here."

* * *

On June 3, Howard got his last intelligence report. Major Schmidt had completed his defenses; his trenches along the canal banks were done, as was the pillbox, and the antitank gun was in place. The garrison consisted of about fifty men armed with six light machine guns, one antiaircraft machine gun, an antitank gun, and a heavy machine gun in its own pillbox. A maze of tunnels connected the underground bunkers and the fighting posts. More buildings had been torn down to open fields of fire. The antiglider poles appeared to have arrived but were not in place yet.

That same day, Monty himself came through Tarrent Rushton. He asked to see the gliders and John Howard. He wanted to know if Major Howard thought he could pull off the coup de main, and he was obviously acquainted with details of the operation. Howard assured him that the job would be done. Monty's parting remark was quiet but moving. "Get as many of the chaps back as you can."

General Gale paid a visit. He gathered his airborne troops around him and gave them his version of an inspirational talk. Jack Bailey can recall only one line: Gale said that "the German today is like the June bride. He knows he is going to get it, but he doesn't know how big it is going to be."

June 4 was to be the day, or rather the evening, to go. D Company was primed for it, aching to get going. Everyone got into battle dress in the afternoon, prepared to go to the gliders. Word came down that the mission was off. Cancellation had been expected, what with the high winds and heavy rains sweeping the countryside, but was still a major disappointment. John Howard wrote in his diary, "The weather's broken—what cruel luck. I'm more downhearted than I dare show. Wind and rain, how long will it last? The longer it goes on, the more prepared the Huns will be, the greater the chance of obstacles on the LZ. Please God it'll clear up tomorrow."

Parr and his gang went to the movies. They saw *Stormy Weather*, featuring Lena Horne and Fats Waller, and rather liked it. The officers gathered in David Wood's room and polished off two bottles of whiskey. Twice Den Brotheridge fell into a depressed mood, and Wood could hear him reciting a poem that began, "If I should die I must . . ." But his spirits soon recovered.

The following morning, June 5, the officers and men checked and rechecked their weapons. At noon, they were told that it was on, that they should rest, eat, and then dress for battle. The meal was fatless, to cut down on airsickness. Not much of it was eaten. Wally Parr explains why: "I think everybody had gone off of grub for the first time possibly in years." Then they sat around, according to Parr, "trying to look so keen, but not too keen like."

Toward evening the men got into their trucks to drive to their gliders. They were a fearsome sight. They each had a rifle or a Sten gun or a Bren gun, six to nine grenades, four Bren-gun magazines. Some had mortars; one in each platoon had a wireless set strapped to his chest. They had all used black cork or burned coke to blacken their faces. (Darky Baines, as he was called, one of the two black men in the company, looked at Parr when Parr handed him some cork and said, "I don't think I'll bother.") Wood remarked that they all, officers and men, were so fully loaded that "if you fell over it was impossible to get up without help." (Each infantryman weighed 250 pounds, instead of the allotted 210.) Parr called out that the sight of them alone would be enough to scare the Germans out of their wits.

As the trucks drove toward the gliders, Billy Gray can remember "the WAFS and the NAAFI girls along the runway, crying their eyes out." On the trucks, the men were given their code words. The recognition signal was "V," to be answered by "for Victory." Code word for the successful capture of the canal bridge was "Ham," for the river bridge "Jam." "Jack" meant the canal bridge had been captured but destroyed; "Lard" meant the same for the river bridge. Ham and Jam. D Company liked the sound of it, and as the men got out of their trucks they began shaking hands and saying, "Ham and Jam, Ham and Jam."

Howard called them together. "It was an amazing sight," he remembers. "The smaller chaps were visibly sagging at the knees under the amount of kit they had to carry." He tried to give an inspiring talk, but as he confesses, "I am a sentimental man at heart, for which reason I don't think I am a good soldier. I found offering my thanks to these chaps a devil of a job. My voice just wasn't my own."

Howard gave up the attempt at inspiration and told the men to load up. The officers shepherded them aboard, although not before every man, except Billy Gray, took a last-minute leak. Wally Parr chalked "Lady Irene" on the side of Wallwork's glider. As the officers fussed over the men outside, those inside their gliders began settling in.

A private bolted out of his glider and ran off into the night. Later, at his court-martial, the private explained that he had had an unshakable premonition of his own death in a glider crash.

The officers got in last. Before climbing aboard, Brotheridge went back to Smith's glider, shook Smith's hand, and said, "See you on the bridge."

Howard went around to each glider, shook hands with the platoon leader, then called out some words of cheer. He had just spoken to the commander of the Halifax squadron, he said, who had told him, "John, don't worry about flak; we are going through a flak gap over Cabourg, one that we have been using to fly supplies in to the Resistance and to bring information and agents out."

Finally Howard, wearing a pistol and carrying a Sten gun, climbed into his own glider, closed the door, and nodded to Wallwork. Wallwork told the Halifax pilot that everything was go. At 2256 hours, June 5, they took off, the other gliders following at one-minute intervals.

At Vimont, east of Caen, Colonel von Luck had just come in from an exercise, and after a bite to eat sat down to do paper work. In Ranville, Major Schmidt enjoyed his wine and his companion. At the canal bridge, Private Bonck thought with relief that there was only an hour to go and he was finished for the night. In the bunker, Private Romer groaned in his sleep, aware that he would have to get up soon to go on duty.

Sergeant Heinz Hickman drove over the bridge, identifying himself to Bonck. He was setting off for the coast to pick up the four young soldiers. As he passed the Gondrée café, he regretted that the curfew was in force. He had stopped in at the place the other day and rather liked it.

At the café, the Gondrées went to bed. In Oxford, Joy Howard did the same. In London's East End, Irene Parr stayed up. She could hear planes gathering, and what she heard sounded bigger than anything she had ever heard before.

5

D-DAY: 0016 TO 0026 HOURS

WALLWORK STRUGGLED WITH his great wooden bird, swooping silently alongside the canal, below the horizon, unseen, unheard. He was trying to control the exact instant at which the Horsa lost its contest with gravity. Wally Parr glanced out the open door and "God Almighty, the trees were doing ninety miles an hour. I just closed my eyes and went up in my guts." Wallwork could see the bridge looming ahead of him, the ground rushing up, trees to his left, a soft, marshy pond to his right. He could see the barbed wire, straight ahead. He was going too fast, and was in danger of plowing up against the road embankment. He was going to have to use the chute, a prospect he dreaded: "We didn't fancy those things at all. We knew they were highly dangerous, nothing but gadgets really, never tested." But if he was to stop in time, he would have to use the chute.

Simultaneously, he was worried about the chute stopping him too quickly and leaving him short of his objective. He wanted to get as far up the LZ as possible, into the barbed wire if he could, "not because Howard wanted me to, not because I was particularly brave or awfully skilled, but because I didn't want to be rear-rammed by number two or number three coming in behind me."

As the wheels touched ground, Wallwork yelled at Ainsworth, "Stream!" Ainsworth pushed the button, the chute billowed out, "and by golly it lifted the tail and shoved the nose wheel down." The whole glider then bounced back up into the air, all three wheels now torn off. "But the chute drew us back, knocked the speed down tremendously, so in two seconds or less I told Ainsworth, 'Jettison,' so Ainsworth pressed the tit and away went the parachutes and we were only going along possibly at sixty miles an hour."

The Horsa hit the ground again, this time on its skids. They threw up hundreds of friction sparks from the rocks; Howard and the other passengers thought these were tracer bullets, that they had been seen and were being fired upon. Suddenly, Howard recalls, "There was the most hellish din imaginable, the most God Almighty crash."

The nose had buried into the barbed wire, and crumbled. The crash sent Wallwork and Ainsworth flying forward, still strapped into their seats, which had broken loose. They went right out the cockpit and onto the ground beneath it. They were thus the first Allied troops to touch French soil on D-Day. Both were, however, unconscious.

Inside the glider, the troops, the sappers, and the company commander were also all unconscious. Howard had broken through his seat belt and was thrown against the roof beams, which jammed his helmet down over his ears and knocked him out.

Save for an occasional low moan, there was complete silence. Private Romer, pacing on the bridge, heard the crash, but assumed it was a piece of wing or tail from a crippled British bomber, a not-unusual occurrence, and went on pacing.

D Company had achieved complete surprise. Wallwork and Ainsworth had taken #1 platoon and set it down where it was supposed to be. Theirs had been a magnificent performance.*

But all their passengers were knocked out. Romer was turning at the west end of the bridge, beginning to pace toward the east. If he noticed the glider sitting there, not fifty yards from the east end of the bridge, and if he gave the alarm, and if the men in the machine-gun pillbox woke quickly enough, #1 platoon would be wiped out inside the Horsa.

To the men in the glider, it seemed afterward that they must have been out for minutes. Each man was struggling to regain consciousness, dimly aware that he had a job to do and that his life was threatened. It seemed to each of them that it was a desperate and time-consuming process to clear the mind and get moving. Minutes, at least, they all recall—three minutes some say, even five minutes according to others.

In fact, they came to within eight to ten seconds. This was the critical moment, the payoff for all those hours, weeks, months, years of training. Their physical fitness paid off first—they shook their collective heads, got rid

*Air Chief Marshal Leigh-Mallory, commanding the Allied air forces on D-Day, called it the greatest feat of flying of World War II.

of the cobwebs, and were alert, eager to go. Few heavyweight boxers could have recovered from such a blow so quickly.

Then their endless training paid off, as they automatically unbuckled, cut their way through the smashed-up door, or hopped out the back. Once again it seemed to Parr, Bailey, Gray, and the others that chaos reigned, that everyone was getting in everyone else's way as they tried to get out. In fact, the exit was smooth and swift.

Howard thought he was dead or blind, until he pushed his helmet up and realized that he could see and that he was all right. He felt a wave of relief, and watched with pride as #1 platoon went through its exit drill. Howard hopped out and saw the bridge looming over him, the barbed wire crushed at his feet. There was no firing. He felt exhilarated. "God bless those pilots," he thought.

Not a word was spoken aloud. Brotheridge got Bailey and told him, whispering in his ear, "Get your chaps moving." Bailey and two others had the task of destroying the machine-gun pillbox. They moved off. Then Brotheridge gathered the remainder of his platoon, whispered, "Come on, lads," and began running for the bridge.

At that moment, glider #2 came down, exactly one minute behind #1. Oliver Boland was the pilot. He could see Wallwork's Horsa ahead of him, "and I didn't want to run up his arse," so Boland used his chute, and hit his spoilers hard, forcing his Horsa onto the ground. He had to swerve to avoid hitting Wallwork's glider; as he did so he broke the back off #2 glider. He stopped right on the edge of the pond, a bit shaken, but conscious. He

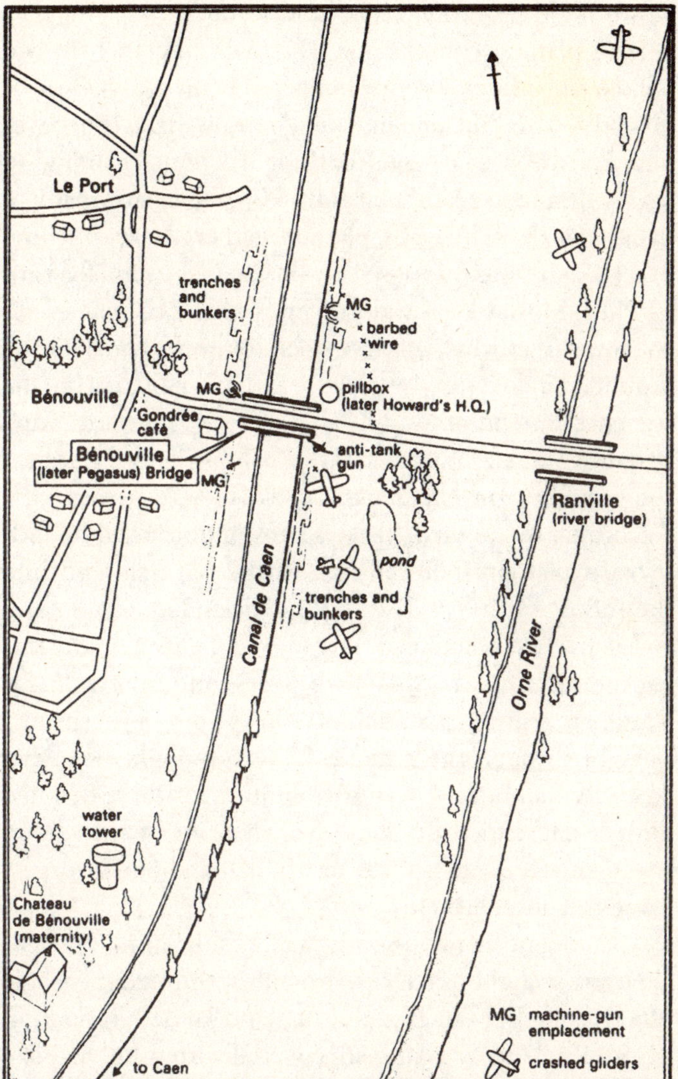

Le Port
trenches and bunkers
MG
barbed wire
Bénouville
MG
pillbox (later Howard's H.Q.)
Gondrée café
Bénouville (later Pegasus) Bridge
MG
anti-tank gun
Ranville (river bridge)
pond
trenches and bunkers
Canal de Caen
Orne River
water tower
Chateau de Bénouville (maternity)
MG machine-gun emplacement
crashed gliders
to Caen

called over his shoulder to his passengers, "We're here, piss off and do what you're paid to do."

The platoon commander, David Wood, was thrown out of the glider by the impact. He had a bucket of grenades with him, and his Sten, bayonet fixed (the bayonets had been sharpened back at Tarrent Rushton, an overly dramatic gesture on John Howard's part, many of his chaps thought). His platoon gathered around him, exactly as it was supposed to do, and he went forward to where Howard was waiting, just by the perimeter wire.

Howard and his wireless operator were lying on the ground, having just been shot at by a rifleman in the trenches on the other side of the road. Howard whispered to Wood, "Number three task." That meant clear the trenches on the northeast side, across the road. According to Howard, "Like a pack of unleashed hounds Wood's platoon followed him across the road and into the fray." As they did so, #3 glider landed.

Like #1, #3 bounced, streamed its chute, and came back down on its skids with a resounding crash. Dr Vaughan, riding just behind the pilots, was thrown straight through the cockpit; his last thought was what a bloody fool he had been to volunteer for these damned gliders. He ended up some feet in front of the glider, really knocked out—it was nearly half an hour before he came to consciousness.

Lieutenant Sandy Smith was beside him. "I went shooting straight past those two pilots, through the whole bloody lot, shot out like a bullet, and landed in front of the glider." He was stunned, covered with mud, had lost his Sten gun, and "didn't really know what the bloody hell I was doing." Pulling himself up on his knees, Smith looked up and into the face of one of his section leaders. "Well," the corporal said quietly, "what are we waiting for, sir?"

"And this," as Smith analyzes the event forty years later, "is where the training comes in." He staggered to his feet, grabbed a Sten gun, and started moving toward the bridge. Half a dozen of his chaps were still trapped inside the crashed glider; one of them drowned in the pond, the only casualty of the landing. It was 0018.

Back in the Bénouville whorehouse, Private Bonck had just unlaced his boots. On the bridge, Private Romer had just passed his fellow sentry at the midpoint and was approaching the eastern end. Brotheridge and his platoon came rushing up the embankment. As the shot aimed at Howard broke the silence, Romer saw twenty-two British airborne troops, appearing so far as he was concerned literally out of nowhere, in their camouflaged battle smocks, their faces grotesquely blacked, giving the most eerie sensation of a blending of savagery and civilization, the civilization half of it represented by the Stens and Brens and Enfields they carried at their hips, ready to fire.

They were coming at Romer at a steady trot, as determined a group as Romer thought he would ever encounter. Romer could see in a flash, by the way the men carried their weapons, by the look in their eyes and by the way their eyes darted around, all white behind the black masks, that they were highly trained killers who were determined to have their way that night. Who was he to argue with them, an eighteen-year-old schoolboy who scarcely knew how to fire his rifle.

Romer turned and ran, back toward the west end, shouting "Paratroopers!" at the other sentry as he passed him. That sentry pulled out his Verey pistol and fired a flare; Brotheridge gave him a full clip from his Sten and cut him down. The first German had just died in defense of Hitler's Fortress Europe.

Simultaneously, Bailey and his comrades tossed grenades into the apertures of the machine-gun pillbox. There was an explosion, then great clouds of dust. When it settled, Bailey found no one living inside. He ran across the bridge, to take up his position near the café.

The sappers, by this time, were beginning to inspect the bridge for explosives, and were already cutting fuses and wires.

Sergeant Hickman was driving into Le Port, had almost arrived at the T-junction, where he would make a left turn to go over the bridge, when he heard Brotheridge's Sten. He told his driver to stop. He knew immediately that it was a Sten—he says today that the Sten and the Bren both had distinctive rates of fire, easily recognizable, and, he adds, both distinctly inferior to their German counterparts. Grabbing his Schmeisser, Hickman motioned to two of his privates to get on the right side of the road leading to the bridge, while he and the other two privates moved down the left side.

Romer's shout, the Verey pistol, and Brotheridge's Sten gun combined to pull the German troops manning the machine-gun pits and the slit trenches on both sides of the bridge into full alert. The privates, all conscripted foreigners, began edging away, but the NCOs, all Germans, opened fire with their MG 34s and their Schmeissers.

Brotheridge, almost across the bridge, pulled a grenade out of his pouch and threw it at the machine gun to his right. As he did so, he was knocked over by the impact of a bullet in his neck. Just behind him, also running, came Billy Gray, his Bren gun at his hip. Billy also fired at the sentry with the Verey pistol, then began firing toward the machine guns. Brotheridge's grenade went off, wiping out one of the gun pits. Gray's Bren, and shots from others crossing the bridge, knocked out the other machine gun.

Gray was standing at the end of the bridge, at the northwest corner. Brotheridge was lying in the middle of the bridge, at the west end. Other men in the section were running onto the bridge. Wally Parr was with them, Charlie Gardner beside him. In the middle of the bridge, Parr suddenly stopped. He was trying to yell "Able, Able," as the men around him had started doing as soon as the shooting broke out. But to his horror, "my tongue was stuck to the roof of my mouth and I couldn't spit sixpence. My mouth had dried up of all saliva and my tongue was stuck."

His attempts to yell only made the sticking worse. Parr's frustration was a terrible thing to behold—Parr without his voice was an impossible thing to imagine. His face was a fiery red, even through the burned cork, from the choking and from his anger. With a great effort of will Parr broke his tongue loose and shouted in his great Cockney voice, "COME OUT AND FIGHT, YOU SQUARE-HEADED BASTARDS," with a very long drawn-out A and the last syllable pronounced "turds." Pleased with himself, Parr started yelling "Ham and Jam, Ham and Jam," as he ran the rest of the way over, then turned left to go after the bunkers that were his task.

The moon emerged from behind the clouds. As it did, Sergeant Hickman had crept to within fifty meters of the bridge. He saw #1 platoon coming over, "and they even frightened me, the way they charged, the way they fired, the way they ran across the bridge. I'm not a coward, but at that moment I got frightened. If you see a para in full pack, they frighten the daylights out of you. And at nighttime when you see a para running with a Bren gun, and the next with a Sten, and no cover round my back, just me and four youngsters who had never been in action, so I could not rely on them—in those circumstances, you get scared. It's my own poor little life there. So I pull my trigger, I fire."

He fired at Billy Gray, reloading his Bren by the corner of the bridge. Billy finished reloading and fired a clip back. Both men were shooting from the hip, and both were pointing their guns just a bit too high, so each sent a full clip over the other man's head. Hickman put another clip into his Schmeisser and started spraying the bridge, as Billy popped into the barn on his right. As soon as he got inside, Billy rested his Bren gun on the wall and took a pee.

Hickman, meanwhile, had run out of ammunition, and besides, he was furious with the bridge garrison, which was hardly putting up a fight at all. He was scornful of such troops—"they had a cushy life, all the war years in France. Never been in danger, only did guard duty." The British, Hickman concluded, "had caught them napping." Hickman decided to get out of there. Motioning to his four privates, he got back in the staff car and sped toward Caen, going the long way around to get to his headquarters, which were only a few kilometers straight east. Thus Hickman was the first German to pay the price for the capture of the bridge—what should have been a ten- or fifteen-minute ride took him six hours (because he had to work his way around bombed-out Caen), and by the time he arrived at his headquarters to report that airborne troops had landed, his major had long since been informed.

As Hickman turned to leave, Smith came running across the catwalk on the south side of the bridge, huffing more than he was running because he had wrenched his knee in the crash. Brotheridge's men were throwing grenades and firing their weapons; there was some German return fire. As Smith got to the other side, he saw a German in the act of throwing a stick grenade at him. As the German turned to leap over the low courtyard wall that ran around the front of the café, Smith gave him a burst with his Sten gun. The German slumped over the wall, dead. Simultaneously the grenade went off. Smith did not feel anything, but his corporal came up to inquire, "Are you all right, sir?" Smith noticed holes in his battle smock and his trousers. Then he looked at his wrist. All the flesh had been torn away, there was nothing but bone. Smith's first thought was "Christ, no more cricket." Curiously, his trigger finger still worked.

Georges Gondrée had wakened at the noise. Crawling on his hands and knees, he got to the window ledge and peered over. Smith looked up from his wrist at the movement, saw Gondrée's head, swung the Sten toward him, and let go a burst. He pointed the Sten too high, so he shattered the window and sent bullets tearing into the wooden beams, but did not hit Gondrée, who beat a hasty retreat, then took his wife and daughters down into the basement.

When Private Bonck heard the first shots, he pulled on his pants, laced up his boots, buttoned his shirt, grabbed his rifle, and dashed out of the whorehouse onto the street. His comrade was already there; together they ran down to the T-junction. After one look at the fire fight going on, they turned and ran back through Bénouville on the road to Caen. When they were out of breath they stopped, talked over the situation, fired off all their ammunition, and then ran back to Bénouville, there to report breathlessly that British troops were on the bridge and that they had expended all their ammunition before hurrying back to report.

At 0019 Brigadier Poett hit the ground, the first of the paratroopers to arrive. He had not been able to orient himself during his short drop, and after a soft landing he undid his harness, gathered himself together, looked around, and realized he did not know where he was. The church tower at Ranville was supposed to be his recognition point, but he was in a little depression in a cornfield and could not see it. Nor could he see any of his chaps. He had set out to find some of his soldiers, especially his wireless operator, when he heard Brotheridge's Sten go off. That fixed his rendezvous point exactly in his mind and he began walking toward it, as fast as a man could move at night through a cornfield. On the way he picked up one private.

Over England, at 0020, Captain Richard Todd's Stirling bomber began to straighten out for its run over the Channel. Todd, twenty-four years old, had set aside a promising acting career to join the paratroopers. Commissioned early in 1941, he was in the 7th Battalion of the 5th Brigade of the 1st Airborne Division. The colonel of the battalion, Jeffery Pine Coffin, was in the same group of Stirling bombers as Todd—the paras were on their way to reinforce the coup de main party at the bridge.

Todd was supposed to fly in Stirling #36, but as his group jumped out of its truck and started to climb aboard the aircraft, a senior RAF officer stepped forward and said he was going along, and that this plane would be #1. "I sort of feebly protested at that," Todd says, "because we had our plan worked out, our jumping plan, but you can't argue with somebody senior to you. I was lucky, in fact, because the first twenty or so aircraft got in with the help of surprise, and when I was down there looking up at the others streaming in, the numbers in the thirties were all getting knocked down. The one that replaced me was knocked down and all the chaps on it were lost, so I had a bit of luck that night."

At 0020 hours, Fox and his platoon had an easy landing, some three hundred meters from the river bridge. According to Fox, the real leader in the platoon was Sergeant Thornton. "He was a remarkable man," Fox says of Wagger Thornton. "In barracks a quiet, unobtrusive man who would as soon sweep the barrack room himself as order a soldier to do it, but in action he was absolutely first-class, and he virtually commanded the platoon. I was the figurehead and did more or less what he told me to do."

When they landed, Thornton reminded Fox that he had forgotten to open the door; when Fox could not get it open, Thornton showed him how to do it. When they got out and formed up, a corporal was supposed to move off with the lead section, Fox following at the head of the other two sections. But the corporal just stood there. Fox approached him to ask what was the matter; the corporal replied that he could see someone with a machine gun up ahead. "To hell with it," responded Fox, "let's get cracking." But the corporal still would not move.

Fox started off himself. There was a burst of fire from an MG 34. Everyone hit the ground. "Then," Fox relates, "dear old Thornton, as quick as ever, had got from way back in his position a mortar going, and he put a mortar, slap down, a fabulous shot, right on the machine gun, so we just rushed the bridge, all the chaps yelling 'Easy, Easy, Easy.'"

They reached the east bank, Lieutenant Fox in the lead. There was no opposition—the sentries had run off when the mortar was fired. As Fox stood there, panting and drinking in his victory, Thornton came up to him. Thornton said he had set up the Bren gun on the inside of the bridge, so that he could cover the advance party. Then he suggested to Fox that it might be a good idea to spread out a bit, instead of standing all bunched together on the end of the bridge. Fox agreed and spread the men out.

At 0021, Sweeney's glider was almost on the ground. Sweeney called out, "Good luck, lads. Don't forget that as soon as we land, we're out and no hesitating." Then he heard the glider pilot say with an oath, "Oh, damn it." The Horsa had hit a slight air pocket and dropped to the ground sooner than the pilot wanted it to. The landing itself was smooth. Turning to Sweeney, the pilot said, "I'm sorry, I've landed about four hundred yards short." Actually, he was more like seven hundred meters short.

The exit was smooth. Sweeney gathered his platoon and set off at a trot. Just that quick he fell into a drainage ditch and was soaked. He got out and started doubling forward. When he and his men reached the bridge, they charged right across, shouting "Fox, Fox, Fox" at the top of their lungs. Because there was no opposition, Sweeney half suspected that either Priday's or Fox's platoon had got there before him, "but I still had that awful feeling as I went over the bridge that the thing might go up under our feet, blown up in our face." He left one section at the west bank, crossing with the other two sections. The men were "thumping along beside me, and Fox was there, his men shouting back 'Easy, Easy, Easy.'

"And so we came to a halt, rather disappointed, because we were all worked up to kill the enemy, bayonet the enemy, be blown up or something, and then there on the other side of the bridge was nothing more than the unmistakable figure of Dennis Fox."

Sweeney had often seen Fox standing just like that on

countless occasions during the practice runs back at Exeter. At those times, Fox's great concern, like that of all the platoon leaders, had always been the umpires and how they would score his performance.

Sweeney raced up to Fox. "Dennis, Dennis, how are you? Is everything all right?"

Fox looked him up and down. "Yes, I think so, Tod," he replied. "But I can't find the bloody umpires."

By 0021, the three platoons at the canal bridge had subdued most resistance from the machine-gun pits and the slit trenches—the enemy had either been killed or run off. Men previously detailed for the job began moving into the bunkers. Sandy Smith remembers that "the poor buggers in the bunkers didn't have much of a chance and we were not taking any prisoners or messing around, we just threw phosphorous grenades down and high-explosive grenades into the dugouts there and anything that moved we shot."

Wally Parr and Charlie Gardner led the way into the bunkers on the left. When they were underground, Parr pulled open the door to the first bunker and threw in a grenade. Immediately after the explosion, Gardner stepped into the open door and sprayed the room with his Sten gun. Parr and Gardner repeated the process twice; then, having cleaned out that bunker, and with their eardrums apparently shattered forever by the concussion and the sound, they went back up to the ground.

Their next task was to meet with Brotheridge, whose command post was scheduled to be the café, and take up firing positions. As they rounded the corner of the café,

Gardner threw a phosphorous grenade toward the sound of sporadic German small-arms fire. Parr shouted at him, "Don't throw another one of those bloody things, we'll never see what's happening."

Parr asked another member of D Company, "Where's Danny?" (To his face, the men all called him "Mr Brotheridge." The officers called him "Den." But the men thought of him and referred to him as "Danny.")

"Where's Danny?" Parr repeated. The soldier did not know, had not seen Lieutenant Brotheridge. "Well," Parr thought, "he's here, Danny must be here somewhere." Parr started to run around the café. "I ran past a bloke lying on the ground in the road opposite the side of the café." Parr glanced at him as he ran on. "Hang on," he said to himself, and went back and knelt down.

"I looked at him, and it was Danny Brotheridge. His eyes were open and his lips moving. I put my hand under his head to lift him up. He just looked. His eyes sort of rolled back. He just choked and he laid back. My hand was covered with blood.

"I just looked at him and thought, 'My God.' Right in the middle of that thing I just knelt there and I looked at him and I thought, 'What a waste!' All the years of training we put in to do this job—it lasted only seconds and he lay there and I thought, 'My God, what a waste.'"

Jack Bailey came running up. "What the hell's going on?" he asked Parr.

"It's Danny," Parr replied. "He's had it."

"Christ Almighty," Bailey muttered.

Sandy Smith, who had thought that everyone was going to be incredibly brave, was learning about war. He was astonished to see one of his best men, a chap he had come to depend heavily on during exercises and who he thought would prove to be a real leader on the other side, cowering in a slit trench, praying. Another of his lads reported a sprained ankle from the crash and limped off to seek protection. He had not been limping earlier. Lieutenant Smith lost a lot of illusions in a hurry.

On the other (east) side of the bridge, David Wood's platoon was clearing out the slit trenches and the bunkers. The task went quickly enough, most of the enemy having run away. Wood's lads were shouting "Baker, Baker, Baker" as they moved along, shooting at any sign of movement in the trenches. Soon they were pronounced clear of enemy. Wood discovered an intact MG 34 with a complete belt of ammunition on it that had not been fired. He detailed two of his men to take over the gun. The remainder of his men filled in the trenches, and Wood went back to report to Howard that he had accomplished his mission.

As he moved back, he was telling his platoon, "Good work, lads," and "Well done," when there was a burst from a Schmeisser. Three bullets hit virtually simultaneously in his left leg, and Wood went down, frightened, unable to move, bleeding profusely.

Wallwork, meanwhile, had come to, lying on his stomach under the glider. "I was stuck. Ainsworth was stuck and I could hear him. I came around. Ainsworth seemed to be in bad shape and yet he would shout. All he could say was 'Jim, are you all right, Jim? Are you all right, Jimmy?' and he was a sight worse than I was, he was pinned under."

Wallwork asked if Ainsworth could crawl out. No. "If I lift it, can you crawl out?" Yes. "And I lifted the thing. I felt like I was lifting the whole bloody glider; I felt like Hercules when I picked this thing up. Ainsworth managed to crawl out." As a medic looked after Ainsworth, Wallwork began to unload ammunition from the glider and carry it forward to the fighting platoons. He did not yet realize that his head and forehead had been badly cut, and that blood was streaking down his face.

Over at the river bridge, Sweeney's section on the far bank heard a patrol coming up the towpath from the direction of Caen. The section leader challenged the patrol with the password, "V." But the answer from the patrol was certainly not "for Victory," and it sounded like German. The entire section opened fire and killed all four men. Later investigation showed that one of them was a British para, one of the pathfinders who had been caught by the German patrol, which evidently was taking the prisoner back to headquarters for interrogation.

By 0022, Howard had set up his command post in a trench on the northeast corner of the bridge. Corporal Tappenden, the wireless operator, was at his side. Howard tried to make out how the fire fight was going at his bridge as he waited for reports from the river bridge. The first information to come to him was nearly devastating: Brotheridge was down.

"It really shook me," Howard says, "because it was Den and how much of a friend he was, and because my leading platoon was now without an officer." The next bit of news was as bad: Wood and his wireless operator and his sergeant were all wounded and out of action. Another runner reported that Lieutenant Smith had about lost his wrist, and had a badly wrenched knee to boot.

All three platoon leaders gone, and in less than ten minutes! Fortunately, the sergeants were thoroughly familiar with the various tasks and could take over; in Wood's platoon, a corporal took charge. In addition, Smith was still on his feet, although hardly mobile and in great pain. Howard had no effective officers at the canal bridge, and did not know what was happening at the river bridge. Gloom might have given way to despair had he known that his second-in-command, Captain Priday, and one-sixth of his fighting strength had landed twenty kilometers away, on the River Dives.

Howard kept asking Tappenden, "Have you heard anything from the river, from numbers four, five, and six?" "No," Tappenden kept replying, "no, no."

Over the next two minutes, there was a dramatic change in the nature of the reports coming in, and consequently in Howard's mood. First Jock Neilson of the sappers came up to him: "There were no explosives under the bridge, John." Neilson explained that the bridge had been prepared for demolition, but the explosives themselves had not been put into their chambers. The sappers removed all the firing mechanisms, then went into the line as infantry. The next day they found the explosives in a nearby shed.

Knowing that the bridge would not be blown was a great relief to Howard. Just as good, the firing was dying down, and from what Howard could see through all the

1 Oblique aerial reconnaissance photograph taken March 24, 1944, showing the river and canal bridge, with the beaches where the landing took place in the distance. Pegasus Bridge is on the left.

2 Overhead aerial reconnaissance photo taken May 30, 1944, showing Pegasus Bridge below the river bridge. The white dots in the surrounding fields are holes dug for "asparagus" antiglider poles.

3 John Howard, 1942.

4 General Omar Bradley awarding Brigader Nigel Poett the Silver Star in recognition of the 5th Parachute Brigade's taking and holding of Pegasus Bridge; June 9, 1944.

5 Captain Brian Priday, second-in-command of D Company.

6 Jim Wallwork, pilot of No. 1 glider.

7 (*above, left*) Joy Howard, 1942.

8 (*above*) John Howard at Brotheridge's grave, Rainville, 1946.

9 (*left*) Lieutneant "Den" Brotheridge, the first Allied soldier killed in action on D-Day.

10 Aircraft towing Horsa glider.

11 Gliders abandoned north of Rainville.

12 No. 1 glider with Pegasus Bridge beyond. Visable on the right is a bit of the barbed-wire fence the pilot, Jim Wallwork, had been asked aim for.

13 No. 1 glider viewed from the the other end, with John Howard leaning agianst it at left. Wallwork escaped without serious injuries, despite the smashed nose of the glider.

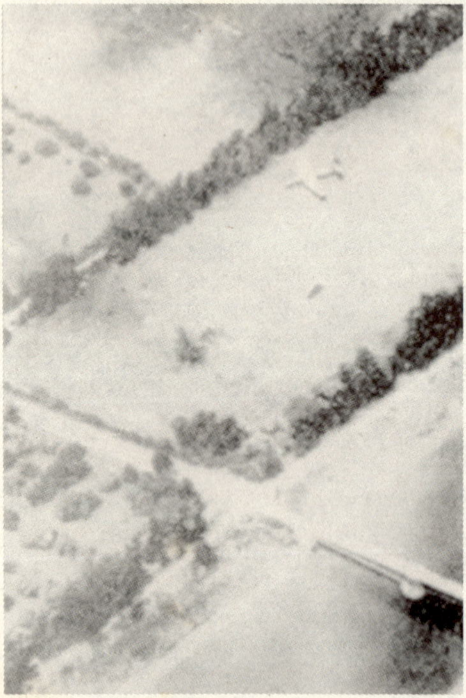

14 (*above*) Aerial-reconnaissance photograph taken at 6 A.M. on D-Day showing three gliders. No. 1 glider is only yards from Pegasus Bridge. The "asparagus" holes are clearly visable in the photograph.

15 Aerial-reconnaissance photograph showing No. 5 glider near the river bridge.

16 Pegasus Bridge with the Gondrée café at left. The German gun used by Wally Parr can be seen in the center of the photograph.

17 Monsieur and Madame Gondrée outside their café. (British time is shown; French time was one hours ahead.)

18 The payoff; a British tank crosses Pegasus Bridge on June 7.

19 Low-level oblique aerial reconnaissance photograph taken March 24, 1944, showing Pegasus Bridge in the center of the picture.

smoke and in the on-again, off-again moonlight, his people had control of both ends of the canal bridge. Just as he realized that he had pulled off Ham, Tappenden tugged at his battle smock. Message coming in from Sweeney's platoon: "We captured the bridge without firing a shot."

Ham *and* Jam! D Company had done it. Howard felt a tremendous exultation, and a surge of pride in his company. "Send it out," he told Tappenden. "Ham and Jam, Ham and Jam, keep it up until you get acknowledgment." Tappenden began incessantly calling out, "Ham and Jam, Ham and Jam."

Tappenden was beaming the message toward the east, hoping that it would be picked up by Brigadier Poett. What he and Howard did not know was that Poett had never found his wireless operator, and was trudging toward them with only one soldier to accompany him.

Hold until relieved. Those were Howard's orders, but one brigadier and one rifleman did not constitute much of a relief.

6

D-DAY: 0026 TO 0600 HOURS

WITH THE BRIDGES captured, Howard's concern shifted from the offense to the defense. He could expect a German counterattack at any time. He was not concerned about the safety of the river bridge, because British paratroopers were scheduled to begin landing around Ranville within one-half hour, and they could take care of protecting that bridge. But to the front of the canal bridge, toward the west, he had no help at all—and a countryside jammed with German troops, German tanks, German lorries. Howard sent a runner over to the river bridge, with orders for Fox to bring his platoon over to the canal bridge. When Fox arrived, Howard intended to push his platoon forward to the T-junction, as the lead platoon.

Howard knew that it would take Fox some time to call his men in from their firing positions, for Sweeney to take over, and for Fox to march the quarter mile from one bridge to the other. But he could already hear tanks starting up in Le Port. They headed south along the road to Bénouville. To Howard's immense relief, the tanks did not turn at the T-junction and come down toward the bridge, but instead continued on into Bénouville. He surmised that the commanders of the garrisons in the two villages were conferring. Howard knew that the tanks would be back.

Tanks coming down the T-junction were by far his greatest worry. With their machine guns and cannons, German tanks could easily drive D Company away from the bridges. To stop tanks, he had only the Piat guns, one per platoon, and the Gammon bombs. Parr came back to the CP from the west end of the bridge to report that he had heard tanks, and to announce that he was going back to the glider for the Piat. "Good man," Howard said.

Parr went down the embankment, climbed into the glider, and "I couldn't see a bloody thing, could I? There was no flashlight. I started scrambling around and at last I found the Piat." Parr picked it up, tripped over some ammunition, sprawled, got up again, and discovered the barrel of the Piat had bent. The gun was useless. Parr threw it down, grabbed some ammunition, and returned to the CP to tell Howard that the Piat was kaput.

Howard yelled at one of Sandy Smith's men to go to his glider and get that Piat. Jim Wallwork trudged by, loaded like a packhorse, carrying ammunition up to the forward platoons. Howard looked at Wallwork's blood-covered face and thought, "That's a strange color camouflage to be wearing at night." To Wallwork, he said, "You look like a bloody red Indian." Wallwork explained about his cuts—by this time, Wallwork thought he had lost his eye—and went about his business.

* * *

At about 0045, Dr Vaughan returned to consciousness. He pulled himself out of the mud, staggered back to the glider, where he could hear one of the pilots moaning, found he could not get the pilot out of the wreckage, and gave him a shot of morphine. Vaughan walked toward the bridge, where he could hear Tappenden calling out, "Ham and Jam, Ham and Jam."

Vaughan stumbled his way to the CP, covered head to toe in mud, mud that stank horribly. He found Howard "sitting in this trench looking perfectly happy, issuing orders right and left."

"Hello, Doc, how are you?" Howard asked.

"All right," Vaughan replied, "but, John, what's all this bloody ham and jam business?"

Howard explained it to him, then told him to look after Brotheridge and Wood, who had been brought by stretcher to a little trench about seventy meters east of the bridge. (When Howard saw Brotheridge being carried past on the stretcher, he could see that it was a fatal wound. "At the top of my mind," Howard says, "was the fact that I knew that Margaret, his wife, was expecting a baby almost any time.")

Vaughan set off for the west end of the bridge. There were shrieks of "Come back, Doc, come back, wrong uniform, unfriendly, wrong way." Howard pointed him toward his destination, the first-aid post in the trench. Before letting the still badly confused Doc wander off again, Howard gave him a shot of whiskey from his flask.

Vaughan finally made it to the aid post, where he found Wood lying on his stretcher. He examined the splint the medical orderly had put on, found it good enough, and gave Wood a shot of morphine. Then he started staggering down the road, again in the wrong direction, again raising cries of "Come back, wrong way, unfriendly."

Returning to the aid post, Vaughan relates, "I found Den lying on his back looking up at the stars and looking terribly surprised, just surprised. And I found a bullet hole right in the middle of his neck." Vaughan gave Brotheridge a shot of morphine and dressed his wound. Shortly thereafter, Brotheridge died. He was the first Allied soldier to be killed by enemy fire on D-Day.

All this time, Tappenden was calling out, "Ham and Jam, Ham and Jam." And as Doc looked after Den, Fox came marching in, in good order. Howard merely told him, "Number five task," and Fox began moving across the bridge. As he passed Smith he got a quick briefing—the tiny bridgehead was secure for the moment, but hostile fire was coming from houses in both Le Port and Bénouville, and tanks had been heard.

Fox remarked that his Piat had been smashed in the landing. "Take mine, old boy," Smith said, handing his Piat to Fox. Fox in turn handed it to Sergeant Thornton. Poor Wagger Thornton was practically buried under equipment by now; a man slightly smaller than average, he had on his pack, his grenade pouch, his Sten gun, magazines for the Bren gun and extra ammunition for himself, and now a Piat gun and two Piat bombs. Overloaded or not, he took the gun and followed Fox forward, toward the T-junction.

At 0040, Richard Todd and his group were over the Channel. Todd was standing over a hole in the bottom of the Stirling bomber, a leg on each side. On each leg, he had a kit bag, one containing a rubber dinghy, the other holding entrenching tools. His Sten was strapped to his chest; he was carrying a pack and a pouch full of grenades and plenty of extra ammunition. Todd's batman stood behind him, holding him and trying to steady him as the Stirling took evasive action from the flak. "Quite a lot of people did fall out over the sea in fact," Todd recalls. "We lost a number of people over the sea from evasive action, who fell out." Todd's batman held tight to him as the Channel slipped past below.

At precisely 0050, exactly on schedule, Howard heard low-flying bombers overhead, at about four hundred feet. To the east and north of Ranville, flares—set by the pathfinders—began to light the sky. Simultaneously, German searchlights from every village in the area went on. Howard recalls the sight: "We had a first-class view of the division coming in. Searchlights were lighting up the chutes and there was a bit of firing going on and you could see tracer bullets going up into the air as they floated down to the ground. It really was the most awe-inspiring sight." Then Howard spoke to the significance of the sight: "Above all, it meant that we were not alone."

Howard began blowing for all he was worth on his metal pea whistle, Dat, Dat, Dat (pause), long Da. It was his prearranged signal, V for Victory. Over and over he blew it, and the sound carried for kilometers in the night air. "Years afterwards," Howard declares, "at reunions and places where paras gather, they'd tell me what a wonderful thing it was to them. Paras who landed alone, in a tree or a bog, in a farmyard, alone, and away from their own friends, could hear that whistle. It not only meant that the bridges had been captured, but it also gave them an orientation."

But it would take the paras at least a half hour, more like an hour, to get to the bridge in any significant numbers; meanwhile, he could still hear tanks rumbling in Bénouville. Wallwork, returning to his glider for another load, went by the CP "and there was Howard, tooting on his bloody whistle and making all sorts of silly noises." Howard stopped blowing long enough to tell Wallwork to get some Gammon bombs up to Fox and his men.

So, Wallwork says, it was "Gammon bombs! Gammon bombs! Gammon bombs! I bowled my flip line. I had already looked for the Gammon bombs once and told Howard that there weren't any Gammon bombs. But he said, 'I put those Gammon bombs on the glider. Get those bloody Gammon bombs,' so back I went panning through this rather badly broken glider looking for Gammon bombs."

Wallwork switched on his flashlight, "and then I heard a sort of rat-tat-tat through the glider. 'What was that?' Rat-tat-tat." A German in a trench down the canal had seen his light and turned his Schmeisser on the glider. "So off went the light, and I thought, 'Howard, you've had your bloody Gammon bombs.'" Wallwork grabbed a load of ammunition and returned to the bridge, reporting to Howard on his way past that there were no Gammon bombs. (No one ever figured out what happened to the Gammon bombs. Wallwork claims that Howard pitched them before takeoff to lighten the load;

Howard claims that they were pinched by the men from #2 and #3 platoons.)

Tappenden kept calling "Ham and Jam." Twice at least he really shouted it out, "Ham and Jam, Ham and BLOODY Jam."

At 0052 the target for Tappenden's message, Brigadier Poett, worked his way through the final few meters of corn and arrived at the river bridge. After checking with Sweeney on the situation there, he walked across to the canal bridge.

Howard's first thought, when he saw his brigadier coming toward him, was "Lieutenant Sweeney's going to get a bloody rocket from me for not letting me know, either by runner or radio, that the brigadier was in the company area." Howard reported while Poett looked around. "Well, everything seems all right, John," Poett said. They crossed the bridge and conferred with Smith. All three officers could hear the tanks and lorries in Bénouville and Le Port; all three knew that if help did not arrive soon, they would lose their precarious hold on the bridge.

At 0052, Richard Todd landed, with other paras dropping all around him. Like Poett earlier, Todd could not get oriented, because he could not see the steeple of the Ranville church. Tracer bullets were flying across the DZ, so he unbuckled and made for a nearby woods, where he hoped to meet other paras and get his bearings. He got them from Howard's whistle.

Major Nigel Taylor, commanding a company of the 7th Battalion of the 5th Brigade, was also confused. The first man he ran into was an officer who had a bugler with him. The two had dropped earlier, with Poett and the pathfinders. Their job was to find the rendezvous in Ranville, then start blowing on the bugle the regimental call of the Somerset Light Infantry. But the officer told Taylor, "I've been looking for this damned rendezvous for three-quarters of an hour, and I can't find it." They ducked into a woods, where they found Colonel Pine Coffin, the battalion commander. He too was lost. They got out their maps, put a flashlight on them, but still could not make out their location. Then they too heard Howard's whistle.

Knowing where Howard was did not solve all Pine Coffin's problems. Fewer than 100 of his more than 350-man force had gathered around him. He knew that Howard had the bridges, but as Nigel Taylor explains, he also knew that "the Germans had a propensity for immediate counterattack. Our job was to get down across that bridge, to the other side. We were the only battalion scheduled to go on that side [west] of the canal. So Pine Coffin's dilemma was, should he move off with insufficient men to do the job, or wait for the battalion to form up. He knew he had to get off as quickly as possible to relieve John Howard." At about 0110, Pine Coffin decided to set off at double time for the bridges, leaving one man to direct the rest of his battalion when it came up.

In Ranville, meanwhile, Major Schmidt had decided he had best investigate all the shooting going on at his bridges. He grabbed one last plateful of food, a bottle of wine, his girl friend, and his driver, summoned his motorcycle escort, and roared off for the river bridge. He was in a big, open Mercedes-Benz. As they sped past his girl friend's house, she screamed that she wanted to be let out. Schmidt ordered the driver to halt, gave her a goodbye pat, and sped on.

The Mercedes came on so fast that Sweeney's men did not have a chance to fire at it before it was already on the bridge. They did open up on the motorcycle that was trailing the car, hit it broadside, and sent it and its driver skidding off into the river. Sweeney, on the west bank, fired his Sten at the speeding Mercedes, riddling it and causing it to run straight off the road. Sweeney's men picked up the driver and Major Schmidt, both badly wounded. In the car they found wine, plates of food, lipstick, stockings, and ladies' lingerie. Sweency had the wounded Schmidt and his driver put on stretchers and carried over to Doc Vaughan's aid post.

By the time he arrived at the post, Schmidt had recovered from his initial shock. He began screaming, in perfect English, that he was the commander of the garrison at the bridge, that he had let his Führer down, that he was humiliated and had lost his honor, and that he demanded to be shot. Alternatively he was yelling that "you British are going to be thrown back, my Führer will see to that; you're going to be thrown back into the sea."

Vaughan got out a syringe of morphine and jabbed him in his butt with it, then set about dressing his wounds. The effect of the morphine, Vaughan reports, "was to induce him to take a more reasonable view of things and after ten minutes of haranguing me about the futility of the Allied attempt to defeat the master race, he relaxed. Soon he was profusely thanking me for my medical attentions." Howard confiscated Schmidt's binoculars.

Schmidt's driver, a sixteen-year-old German, had had one leg blown off. The other leg was just hanging—Vaughan removed it with his scissors. Within a half hour, the boy was dead.

By 0115, Howard had completed his defensive arrangements at the canal bridge. He had Wood's platoon with him at the east end, along with the sappers. He had organized the sappers into a platoon that he was holding in reserve, near his CP. On the west side, Brotheridge's platoon held the café and the ground around it, while Smith's platoon held the bunkers to the right. Smith was in command of both platoons, but he was growing increasingly groggy, due to the loss of blood and the intense pain in his knee, which had started to stiffen. Fox was up ahead, toward the T-junction, with Thornton carrying the only working Piat. The paras of the 7th Battalion were on their way, but their arrival time—and in what strength—was problematical.

Howard could hear the tanks. He was desperate to establish radio communication with Fox, but could not. Then he saw a tank swing slowly, ever so slowly, toward the bridge, its great cannon sniffing the air like the trunk of some prehistoric monster. "And it wasn't long before we could see a couple of them about twenty-five yards apart moving very, very slowly, quite obviously not knowing what to expect when they got down to the bridges."

Everything was now at stake and hung in the balance. If the Germans retook the canal bridge, they would then drive on to overwhelm Sweeney's platoon at the river bridge. There they could set up a defensive perimeter, bolstered by tanks, so strong that the 6th Airborne Division would find it difficult, perhaps impossible, to break through. In that case, the division would be isolated, without antitank weapons to fight off von Luck's armor. It sounds overly dramatic to say that the fate of the more than ten thousand fighting men of the 6th Airborne depended on the outcome of the forthcoming battle at the bridge, but we know from what happened to the 1st Airborne in September 1944 at Arnhem that that was in fact exactly the case.

Beyond the possible loss of the 6th Airborne, it stretches matters only slightly to state that the fate of the invasion as a whole was at risk on John Howard's bridge. We have the testimony of von Luck himself on this subject. He contends that if those bridges had been available to him, he could have crossed the Orne waterways and thrown his regiment into the late-afternoon D-Day counterattack. That attack, by the 192d Regiment of 21st Panzer, almost reached the beaches. Von Luck feels that had his regiment also been in that attack, 21st Panzer would have surely driven to the beaches. A panzer division loose on the beaches, amidst all the unloading going on, could have produced havoc with unimaginable results.

Enough speculation. The point has been made—a great deal was at stake up there at the T-junction. Fittingly, as so much was at stake, the battle at the bridge at 0130 on D-Day provided a fair test of the British and German armies of World War II. Each side had advantages and disadvantages. Howard's opponents were the company commanders in Bénouville and Le Port. Like Howard, they had been training for more than a year for this moment. They had been caught by surprise, but the troops at the bridge had been their worst troops, not much of a loss. In Bénouville, the 1st Panzer Engineering Company of the 716th Infantry Division, and in Le Port, the 2d Engineers, were slightly better quality troops. The whole German military tradition, reinforced by orders, compelled them to launch an immediate counterattack. They had the platoons to do it with, and the armored vehicles. What they did not have was a sure sense of the situation, because they kept getting conflicting reports.

Those conflicting reports were one of the weaknesses of the German Army in France. They came about because of the language difficulties. The officers could not understand Polish or Russian, the men could not understand German. The larger problem was the presence of so many conscripted foreigners in their companies, which in turn was a reflection of Germany's most basic problem in World War II. Germany had badly overreached itself. Its population was insufficient to provide all the troops required on the various fronts. Filling the trenches along the Atlantic Wall with what amounted to slaves from Eastern Europe looked good on paper, but in practice such soldiers were nearly worthless.

On the other hand, German industry did get steady production out of slave labor. Germany had been able to provide its troops with the best weapons in the world, and in abundance. By comparison, British industrial output was woefully inferior, in both quantity and quality.

But although his firearms were inferior, Howard was commanding British troops, every one of them from the United Kingdom and every man among them a volunteer who was superbly trained. They were vastly superior to their opponents. Except for Fox and the crippled Smith, Howard was without officers, but he personally enjoyed one great advantage over the German commanders. He was in his element, in the middle of the night, fresh, alert, capable of making snap decisions, getting accurate reports from his equally fresh and alert men. The German commanders were confused, getting conflicting reports, tired, and sleepy. Howard had placed his platoons exactly where he had planned to put them, with three on the west side to meet the first attacks, two in reserve on the east side (including the sappers), and one at the river bridge. Howard had seen to it that his antitank capability was exactly where he had planned to put it, right up at the T-junction. The German commanders, by way of contrast, were groping, hardly sure of where their own platoons were, unable to decide what to do.

But, as noted, the Germans had the great advantage of badly outgunning Howard. They had a half-dozen tanks to his zero. They had two dozen lorries, and a platoon to fill each one, to Howard's six platoons and no lorries. They had artillery, a battery of 88-mms, while Howard had none. Howard did not even have Gammon bombs. Hand-thrown grenades were of little or no use against a tank, because they usually bounced off and exploded harmlessly in the air. Bren and Sten guns were absolutely useless against a buttoned-down tank. The only weapon Howard had to stop those tanks was

Sergeant Thornton's Piat gun. That gun, and the fact that he had trained D Company for precisely this moment, the first contact with tanks. He felt confident that Thornton was at the top of his form, totally alert, not the least bothered by the darkness or the hour, and that Thornton was fully proficient in the use of a Piat, that he knew precisely where he should hit the lead tank to knock it out.

Others were not quite so confident. Sandy Smith recalls "hearing this bloody thing, feeling a sense of absolute terror, saying, 'My God, what the hell am I going to do with these tanks coming down the road?'" Billy Gray, who had taken up a position in an unoccupied German gun pit, remembers: "Then the tank came down the road. We thought that was it, you know, no way were we going to stop a tank. It was about twenty yards away from us, because we were up on this little hillock, but it did give a sort of field of fire straight up the road. We fired up the road at anything we could see moving."

Gray was tempted to fire at the tank. Most men in their first hour of combat would have done so. But, Gray says, paying a tribute to his training, "I didn't fire at the tank." Gray, along with all Howard's men on the west side of the bridge, held fire. They did not, in short, reveal their positions, thus luring the tanks into the killing zone.

Howard had expected the tanks to be preceded by an infantry reconnaissance patrol—that was the way he would have done it—but the Germans had neglected to do so. Their infantry platoons were following the two tanks. So the tanks rolled forward, ever so slowly, the tankers unaware that they had already crossed the front line.

The first Allied company in the invasion was about to meet the first German counterattack. It all came down to Thornton and the German tankers. The tankers' visibility was such that they could not see Thornton, half buried as he was under that pile of equipment. Thornton was about thirty yards from the T-junction, and, he says, "I don't mind admitting it, I was shaking like a bloody leaf!" He could hear the tank coming toward him. He fingered his Piat.

"The Piat actually is a load of rubbish, really," Thornton says today. "The range is around about fifty yards and no more. You're a dead loss if you try to go farther. Even fifty yards is stretching it, very much so. Another thing is that you must never, never miss. If you do, you've had it, because by the time you reload the thing and cock it, which is a bloody chore on its own, everything's gone, you're done. It's indoctrinated into your brain that you mustn't miss."

Thornton had taken his position as close to the T-junction as he could get, because he wanted to shoot at the shortest possible distance. "And sure enough, in about three minutes, this bloody great thing appears. I was more hearing it than seeing it, in the dark; it was rattling away there, and it turned out to be a Mark IV tank coming along pretty slowly, and they hung around for a few seconds to figure out where they were. Only had two of the bombs with me. Told myself, 'You mustn't miss.' Anyhow, although I was shaking, I took an aim and bang, off it went."

The tank had just turned at the T-junction. "I hit him

round about right bang in the middle. I made sure I had him right in the middle. I was so excited and so shaking I had to move back a bit."

Then all hell broke loose. The explosion from the Piat bomb penetrated the tank, setting off the machine-gun clips, which started setting off grenades, which started setting off shells. As Glen Gray points out in his book *The Warriors*, one of the great appeals of war is the visual display of a battlefield, with red, green, or orange tracers skimming about, explosions going off here and there, flares lighting up portions of the sky. But few warriors have ever had the opportunity to see such a display as that at the T-junction on D-Day.

The din, the light show, could be heard and seen by paratroopers many kilometers from the bridge. Indeed, it provided an orientation and thus got them moving in the right direction.

When the tank went off, Fox took protection behind a wall. He explains, "You couldn't go very far because whizbang a bullet or shell went straight past you, but finally it died down, and incredibly we heard this man crying out. Ole Tommy Klare couldn't stand it any longer and he went straight out up to the tank and it was blazing away and he found the driver had got out of the tank still conscious, was laying beside it, but both legs were gone. He had been hit in the knees getting out, and Klare, who was always kind, he was an immensely strong fellow—back in barracks he once broke a man's jaws by just one blow for getting on his nerves—and Tommy hunched this poor old German on his back and took him to the first-aid post. I thought it was useless of course, but, in fact, I believe the man lived." He did, but only for a few more hours. He turned out to be the commander of the 1st Panzer Engineering Company.

The fireworks show went on and on—all told it lasted for more than an hour—and it helped convince the German company commanders that the British were present in great strength. Indeed, the lieutenant in the second tank withdrew to Bénouville, where he reported that the British had six-pounder antitank guns at the bridge. The German officers decided that they would have to wait until dawn and a clarification of the situation before launching another counterattack. John Howard had won the battle of the night.

Through the night, the lead tank smoldered, right across the T-junction, thus blocking movement between Bénouville and Le Port, and between Caen and the coast. An argument can therefore be made that Sergeant Thornton had pulled off the single most important shot of D-Day, because the Germans badly needed that road. Thornton himself is impatient with any such talk. When I had completed my interview with him, and had shut off the tape recorder, he remarked: "Whatever you do in this book, don't go making me into a bloody hero." To which I could only think to reply, "Sergeant Thornton, I don't make heroes. I only write about them."

By the time the tank went up, at about 0130 hours, Poett's men of the 5th Para Brigade, led by Pine Coffin's 7th Battalion, with Nigel Taylor's company leading the way, were double-timing toward the bridge—at less than one-third strength. The paras knew they were late, because they thought from the fireworks that Howard was undergoing intensive attacks. But, as Taylor explains, "It's very difficult to double in the dark carrying a heavy weight on uneven ground."

When they got on the road leading to the bridges, they ran into Brigadier Poett, who was headed back toward his CP in Ranville. "Come on, Nigel," Poett called out to Taylor in his high-pitched voice. "Double, double, double." Taylor rather thought the order superfluous, but in fact his chaps did break into "a rather shambling run."

Richard Todd was in the group. He recalls the paratrooper medical officer catching up with him, grabbing him by the arm, and saying, "Can I come with you? You see I'm not used to this sort of thing." Todd says that the doctor "was rather horrified because we passed a German who had had his head shot off, but his arms and legs were still waving about and strange noises were coming out of him, and I thought even the doctor was a bit turned over by that."

Todd remembers thinking, as he was running between the river and the canal bridges, " 'Now we're really going into it,' because there was a hell of an explosion and a terrific amount of firing, and tracers going in all directions. It really looked like there was a real fight going on." Major Taylor thought, "Oh, Lord, I'm going to have to commit my company straight into battle on the trot."

When 7th Battalion arrived at the bridge, Howard gave the leaders a quick briefing. The paras then went across, Nigel Taylor's company moving out to the left, into Bénouville, while the other companies moved right, into Le Port. Richard Todd took up his position on a knoll just below the little church in Le Port, while Taylor led his company to prearranged platoon positions in Bénouville. Taylor recalls that, except for the tank exploding in the background, within the hour "everything was absolutely dead quiet." The Germans had hunkered down to await the outcome of the "battle" at the T-junction.

A German motorcycle started up. The driver came around the corner, headed for the T-junction. Taylor's men were on both sides of the road, "and they've been training for God knows how many years to kill Germans, and this is the first one they've seen." They all opened up. As the driver went into shock from the impact of a half-dozen or more bullets, his big twin-engined BMW bike flipped over and came down on him. The throttle was stuck on full, and the bike was in gear. "It was absolutely roaring its head off, and every time it hit the ground, the thing was bucking. shying about." The bike struck one of Taylor's men, causing injuries that later resulted in death, before someone finally got the engine shut off. It was about 0230 hours.

At 0300 hours, Howard got a radio message from Sweeney, saying that Pine Coffin and his battalion headquarters were crossing the river bridge, headed toward the canal. Howard immediately started walking east, and met Pine Coffin halfway between the bridges. They walked back to the canal together, Howard telling Pine Coffin what had happened and what the situation was, so that by the time they arrived at the canal bridge Pine Coffin was already in the picture.

As he crossed the bridge, Pine Coffin queried Sergeant Thornton. Nodding toward the burning tank, the colonel asked, "What the bloody hell's going on up there?"

"It's only a bloody old tank going off," Thornton replied, "but it is making an awful racket."

Pine Coffin grinned. "I should say so," he said. Then he turned left, to make his headquarters on an embankment facing the canal, right on the edge of Bénouville near the church.

After unloading the Horsa he had flown in as #2 glider pilot, Sergeant Boland went off exploring. He headed south, walking beside and below the towpath, and got to the outskirts of Caen. His may have been the deepest penetration of D-Day, although as Boland points out, there were scattered British paras dropping all around him, and some of the paras possibly came down even closer to Caen. At any event, it would be some weeks before British and Canadian forces got that far again.

Boland continues: "I decided I had better go back because it was bloody dangerous, not from the Germans but from bloody paras who were a bit trigger-happy. They'd landed all over the place, up trees, God knows where, and were very susceptible to firing at anybody coming from that direction." After establishing his identity by using the password, Boland led a group of paras back to the bridge.

When he arrived, he saw Wallwork sitting on the bank. "How are you, Jim?" he asked.

Wallwork looked past Boland, saw the paras, and went into a rocket. "Where have you been till now?" he demanded. "We'd all thought you were on a forty-eight-hour pass. The bloody war is over."

"The paras thought they were rescuing us," Boland says. "We felt we were rescuing them."

The arrival of the 7th Battalion freed D Company from its patrolling responsibilities on the west bank and allowed Howard to pull his men back to the ground between the two bridges, where they were held as a reserve company.

When Wally Parr arrived, he set to examining the anti-tank gun emplacement, which had been unmanned when the British arrived and unnoticed since. Parr discovered a labyrinth of tunnels under the emplacement. He got a flashlight, another private, and began exploring. He discovered sleeping quarters. There was nothing in the first two compartments he checked. In the third, he saw a man in bed, shaking violently. Parr slowly pulled back the blanket. "There was this young soldier lying there in full uniform and he was shaking from top to toe, absolutely shaking." Parr got him up with his bayonet, then took him up onto the ground and put him in the temporary POW cage. He returned to the gun pit, where he was joined by Billy Gray, Charlie Gardner, and Jack Bailey.

On his side of the bridge, across the road, Sergeant Thornton had persuaded Lieutenant Fox that there were indeed Germans still sleeping deep down in the dugouts. They set off together, with a flashlight, to find them. Thornton took Fox to a rear bunkroom, opened the door, and shone his light on three Germans, all snoring, with their rifles neatly stacked in the corner. Thornton removed the rifles, then covered Fox with his Sten while Fox shook the German in the top bunk. He snored on.

Fox ripped off the blanket, shone his torch in the man's face, and told him to get up.

The German took a long look at Fox. He saw a wild-eyed young man, dressed in a ridiculous smock, his face blackened, pointing a little toy gun at him. He concluded that one of his buddies was playing a small joke. He told Fox, in German, but in a tone of voice and with a gesture that required no translation, "Fuck off." Then he turned over and went back to sleep.

"It took the wind right out of my sails," Fox admits. "Here I was, a young officer, first bit of action, first German I had seen close up; and giving him an order and receiving such a devastating response—well, it was a bit deflating." Thornton, meanwhile, got to laughing so hard he was crying. He collapsed on the floor, roaring with laughter.

Fox looked at him. "The hell with this," the lieutenant said to the sergeant. "You take over."

Fox went back up to ground level. Shortly thereafter, Thornton brought him a prisoner who spoke a bit of English. Thornton suggested that Fox might like to interrogate him. Fox began asking him about his unit, where other soldiers were located, and so on. But the German ignored his questions. Instead, he demanded to know, "Who are you? What are you doing here? What is going on?"

Fox tried to explain that he was a British officer and that the German was a prisoner. The German could not believe it. "Oh, come on, you don't mean—you can't—Well, how did you land? We didn't hear you land. I mean, where did you come from?" Poor Fox suddenly realized that he was the one being interrogated, and turned the proceedings back over to Thornton, but not before admiring photographs of the prisoner's family.

Von Luck was furious. At 0130 hours, he received the first reports of British paratroopers in his area. He immediately put his regiment on full alert. Locally, he counted on his company commanders to launch their own counterattacks wherever the British had captured a position, but the bulk of the regiment he ordered assembled northeast of Caen. The assembly went smoothly enough, and by 0300 von Luck had gathered his men and their tanks and their SPVs, all together an impressive force. The officers and men were standing beside their tanks and vehicles, engines running, ready to go.

But although von Luck had prepared for exactly this moment, knew where he wanted to go, in what strength, over what routes, with what alternatives, he could not give the order to go. Because of the jealousies and complexities of the German high command, because Rommel disagreed with Rundstedt, because Hitler was contemptuous of his generals and did not trust them to boot, the German command structure was a hopeless muddle. Without going into the details of such chaos, it suffices to note here that Hitler had retained personal control of the armored divisions. They could not be used in a counterattack until he had personally satisfied himself that the action was the real invasion. But Hitler was sleeping, and no one ever liked to wake him, and besides, the reports coming in to the OKW were confused and contradictory, and in any case hardly alarming enough to suggest that this was the main invasion. A nighttime paratrooper drop might just be a diversion. So no order came to von Luck to move out.

"My idea," von Luck explained forty years later, while studying a map, "was, after I got more information about the parachute landings, and the gliders, my idea was that a night attack would be the right way to counterattack, starting at three o'clock or four o'clock in the morning, before the British could organize their defenses, before their air force people could come, before the British Navy could hit us. We were quite familiar with the ground and I think that we could have been able to get through to the bridges."

Pointing at the map, he continued, "I think we could have gotten through around here, even north around here, to cut Major Howard's men from the main body of the landings." And then, von Luck continues, "The whole situation on the east side of the bridges would have been different. The paratroopers would have been isolated and I would have had communications with the other half of the 21st Panzer Division."

But von Luck could not act on his own initiative, so there he sat, a senior officer in an army that prided itself on its ability to counterattack, a leader in one of the divisions Rommel most counted upon to lead the D-Day counterattack, personally quite certain of what he could accomplish, his attack routes all laid out—there he sat, rendered immobile by the intricacies of the leadership principle in the Third Reich.

The Gondrées too were immobilized, inside their café. They were hiding in the cellar. Thérèsa, shivering in her nightdress, urged Georges to return to the ground floor and investigate. "I am not a brave man," he later admitted, "and I did not want to be shot, so I went upstairs on all fours and crawled to the first-floor window. There I heard talk outside but could not distinguish the words, so I pushed open the window and peeped out cautiously. I saw in front of the café two soldiers sitting near my petrol pump with a corpse between them."

Georges was seen by one of the paras. "*Vous civile?*" the soldier kept asking. Georges tried to assure him that he was indeed a civilian, but the man did not speak French and Georges, not knowing what was going on, did not want to reveal the fact that he understood English. He tried some halting German but that got nowhere, and he returned to the cellar to await daylight and developments.

At about 0500, Sandy Smith's knee had stiffened to the point of near-uselessness, his arm had swollen to more than twice normal size, his wrist was throbbing with pain. He approached Howard and said he thought he ought to go over to Doc Vaughan's first-aid post and have his wounds and injuries looked after. "Must you go?" asked Howard plaintively. Smith promised that he would be back in a minute. When he got to the post, Doc Vaughan wanted to give him morphine. Smith refused. Vaughan said he could not go back to duty anyway, because he would be more of a nuisance than a help. Smith took the morphine.

Thus when Howard called for a platoon leader's meeting at his CP, just before dawn, the full weight of the officer loss he had suffered struck him directly. Brotheridge's #1 platoon was being commanded by

Corporal Kane; the sergeant was out of action and the lieutenant dead. Both Wood's and Smith's #2 and #3 platoons were also commanded by corporals. The second-in-command, Brian Priday, and the #4 platoon leader, Tony Hooper, had not been heard from. Only #5 (Fox) and #6 platoons (Sweeney) had their full complement of officers and NCOs. There had been a dozen casualties total, plus two dead.

Howard had not called his platoon leaders together to congratulate them on their accomplishment, but rather to prepare for the future. He went through various counterattack routes and possibilities with them, in the event the Germans broke through the lines of the 7th Battalion. Then he told them to have everyone stand to until first light. At dawn, half the men could stand down and try to catch some sleep.

As the sky began to brighten, the light revealed D Company in occupation of the ground between the two bridges. It had carried out the first part of its mission.

The Germans wanted the bridges back, but their muddled command structure was hurting them badly. At 0300, von Luck had ordered the 8th Heavy Grenadier Battalion, which was one of his forward units located north of Caen and on the west side of the Orne waterways, to march to Bénouville and retake the bridge. But, as Lieutenant Werner Kortenhaus reports, despite its name, the 8th Heavy Grenadier Battalion had with it only its automatic weapons, some light antiaircraft guns, and some grenade launchers. No armor. Nevertheless, the Grenadiers attacked, inflicting casualties on Major Taylor's company and driving it back into the middle of Bénouville. The Grenadiers then dug in "and waited for the arrival of panzers from Twenty-first Panzer Division."

Lieutenant Kortenhaus, who stood beside his tank, engine running, recalls his overwhelming thought over the last two hours of darkness: "Why didn't the order to move come? If we had immediately marched we would have advanced under cover of darkness." But Hitler was still sleeping, and the order did not come.

7

D-DAY: 0600 TO 1200 HOURS

GEORGES GONDRÉE, IN his cellar, welcomed "the wonderful air of dawn coming up over the land." Through a hole in the cellar he could see figures moving about. "I could hear no guttural orders, which I always associated with a German working party," Gondrée later wrote. He asked Thérèsa to go to the hole and listen to the soldiers talk, to determine whether they were speaking German or not. She did so and presently reported that she could not understand what they were saying. Then Georges listened again, "And my heart began to beat quicker for I thought I heard the words 'all right.'"

Members of the 7th Battalion began knocking at the door. Gondrée decided to go up and open it before it was battered down. He admitted two men in battle smocks, with smoking Sten guns and coal-black faces. They asked, in French, whether there were any Germans in the house. He answered "No" and took them into the bar and thence, with some reluctance on their part, which he overcame with smiles and body language, to the cellar. There he pointed to his wife and two children.

"For a moment there was silence," Gondrée wrote. "Then one soldier turned to the other and said, 'It's all right, chum.' At last I knew that they were English and burst into tears." Thérèsa began hugging and kissing the paratroopers, laughing and crying at the same time. As she kissed all the later arrivals too, by midday her face was completely black. Howard remembers that "she remained like that for two or three days afterward, refusing to clear it off, telling everybody that this was from the British soldiers and she was terribly proud of it."

Forty years later, Mme. Gondrée remained the number-one fan of the British 6th Airborne Division. No man who was there on D-Day has ever had to pay for a drink at her café since, and many of the participants have been back often. The Gondrées were the first family to be liberated in France, and they were generous in expressing their gratitude ever after.

Free drinks for the British airborne chaps began immediately upon liberation, as Georges went out into his garden and dug up ninety-eight bottles of champagne that he had buried in June 1940, just before the Germans arrived. Howard describes the scene: "There was a helluva lot of cork-popping went on, enough so that it was heard on the other side of the canal." Howard was on the café side of the bridge, consulting with Pine Coffin. The café had by then been turned into the battalion aid post. So, Howard says, "By the time I got back I was told that everybody wanted to report sick at the aid post. Well, we stopped that lark, of course." Then

Howard confesses, "Well, I didn't go back until I had had a sip, of course, of this wonderful champagne." A bit embarrassed, he explains: "It really was something to celebrate."

Shortly after dawn, the seaborne invasion began. The largest armada ever assembled, nearly six thousand ships of all types, lay off the Norman coast. As the big guns from the warships pounded the beaches, landing craft moved forward toward the coastline, carrying the first of the 127,000 soldiers who would cross the beaches that day. Overhead, the largest air force ever assembled, nearly five thousand planes of all types, provided cover. It was a truly awesome display of the productivity of American, British, and Canadian factories, its like probably never to be seen again. (Ten years later, when he was President of the United States, Eisenhower said that another Overlord was impossible, because such a buildup of military strength on such a narrow front would be far too risky in the nuclear age—one or two atomic bombs would have wiped out the entire force.)

The invasion stretched for some sixty miles, from Sword Beach on the left to Utah Beach on the right. German resistance was spotty, almost nonexistent at Utah Beach, quite effective and indeed almost decisive at Omaha Beach, determined but not irresistible at the British and Canadian beaches, where unusually high tides compressed the landings into narrow strips and added greatly to the problems of German artillery and small-arms fire. Whatever the problems, except at Omaha the invading forces overcame the initial opposition, and a firm lodgment was made. On the far left, in the fighting closest to Howard and D Company, a bitter battle was under way in Ouistreham. Progress toward Caen was delayed.

Howard describes the invasion from D Company's point of view: "The barrage coming in was quite terrific. It was as though you could feel the whole ground shaking toward the coast, and this was going on like hell. Soon afterward it seemed to get nearer. Well, they were obviously lifting the barrage farther inland as our boats and craft came in, and it was very easy, standing there and hearing all this going on and seeing all the smoke over in that direction, to realize what exactly was happening and keeping our fingers crossed for those poor buggers coming by sea. I was very pleased to be where I was, not with the seaborne chaps."

He quickly stopped indulging in sympathy for his seaborne comrades because, with full light, sniper activity picked up dramatically. Suddenly the easy movement back and forth over the bridge became highly dangerous. The general direction of the fire was coming from the west bank, toward Caen, where there was a heavily wooded area and two dominant buildings, the château that was used as a maternity hospital, and the water tower. Where any specific sniper was located, D Company could not tell. But the snipers had the bridge under a tight control, if not a complete grip, and they were beginning to snipe the first-aid post, in its trench beside the road, where Vaughan and his aides were wearing Red Cross bands and obviously tending wounded.

David Wood, who was lying on a stretcher, three

bullets in his leg, recalls that the first sniper bullet hit the ground "a little distance from me, and I thought that I was going to get it next. And then there was a shot which was far too close for comfort, thudded into the ground right next to my head, and I looked up to see that my medical orderly had drawn his pistol to protect his patient, and had accidentally discharged it and very nearly finished me off."

Smith was having his wrist bandaged by another orderly. He relates: "I was sitting in this ditch with my head above it and he was doing my wrist, and then he stood up and one of the snipers shot him straight through the chest, knocked him absolutely miles backwards—the impact, you know. He went absolutely hurtling across the road, landed on his back, screaming, 'Take my grenades out, take my grenades out.' He was frightened of being shot again, with grenades in his pouches." Someone got the grenades out, and he survived, but Smith remembers the incident "as a very low point in my life. I remember also, I thought the next bullet was going to come for me. I felt terrible." Vaughan, bending over a patient, looked up in the direction of the sniper, shook his fist, and declared, "This isn't cricket."

Later that morning, Wood and Smith were evacuated to a regimental aid post in Ranville, where they were also shot at and had to be moved again.

Parr, Gardner, Gray, and Bailey were in the gun pit, trying to figure out how the antitank gun worked. Howard had trained them on German small arms, mortars, machine guns, and grenades, but not on artillery. "We started figuring it out," Parr recalls, "and we got the breech out, all the ammo you want downstairs, brought one shell up, put it in, closed the breech, now, How do you fire it? All right, it's got a telescopic sight on it; it's got a range chart on the side with various points along the canal bank sighted in, one thing and another."

The four soldiers were standing in the gun pit. Because of its camouflage, the snipers could not get at them. They talked it over, trying to locate the firing mechanism. Parr continues: "Charlie Gardner said, 'What's this?' It was a push button. He just pushed it and there was the biggest explosion, the shell screamed off in the general direction of Caen, and, of course, the case shot out of the back and if anybody had stood there it would have caved their ribs in. That's how we learned to fire the gun."

After that, Parr gleefully admits, "I had the time of my life firing that gun." He and his mates were certain that the sniping was coming from the roof of the château. Parr began putting shells through the top floor of the building, spacing them along. There was no discernible decrease in the volume of sniper fire, however, and the snipers' locations remain, forty years later, a mystery.

Parr kept shooting. Jack Bailey tired of the sport and went below, to brew up his first cup of tea of the day. Every time Parr fired, the chamber filled with dust and smoke, and loose sand came shaking down. Bailey called up, "Now, Wally, no firing now, just give me three minutes." Bailey took out his Tommy cooker, lit it, watched as the water came to a boil, shivered with pleasure as he thought how good that tea was going to taste, had his sugar ready to pop into it, when suddenly, "Blam." Wally had fired again. Dust, soot, and sand filled Bailey's mug of tea, and his Tommy cooker was out.

Bailey, certain Wally had timed it deliberately, came tearing up, looking—according to Parr—"like a bloody lunatic." Bailey threatened Parr with immediate dismemberment, but at heart Bailey was a gentle man, and by keeping the gun between himself and Bailey, Parr survived.

Howard dashed across the road, bending low, to find out what Parr was doing. When he realized that Parr was shooting at the château, he was horrified. Howard ordered Parr to cease fire immediately, then explained to him that the château was a maternity hospital. "So," Parr says today, with a touch of chagrin, "that was the first and only time I've ever shelled pregnant women and newborn babies."*

Howard never did convince Parr that the Germans were not using the roof for sniping. As Howard returned to his CP, he called out, "Now you keep that bloody so-and-so quiet, Parr, just keep it quiet."

"Yes, sir."

"Only fire when necessary, and that doesn't mean at imaginary snipers."

"Yes, sir."

* After the war, Parr was reading a magazine article on German atrocities in occupied Europe. He came across a prime example of German bestiality: It seemed, according to the article, that before they withdrew from Bénouville, the Germans had decided to give the village a lesson and proceeded to methodically shell the maternity hospital and ancient château!

Soon Parr was shooting into the trees. Howard yelled, "For Christ's sake, Parr, will you shut up! Will you keep that bloody gun quiet! I can't think over it." Well, Parr thought to himself, "Nobody told me it was going to be a quiet war." But he and his mates stopped firing and started cleaning up the shell casings scattered through the gun pit. It had suddenly occurred to them that if someone slipped on a casing while he was carrying a shell, and if the shell fell point downward into the brimful ammunition room, they and their gun and the bridge itself would all go sky-high.

By 0700, the British 3d Division was landing at Sword Beach, and the big naval gunfire had lifted to start pounding Caen, en route passing over D Company's position. "They sounded so big," Howard says, "and being poor bloody infantry, we had never been under naval fire before and these damn great shells came sailing over, such a size that you automatically ducked, even in the pillbox, as one went over, and my radio operator was standing next to me, very perturbed about this, and finally Corporal Tappenden said, 'Blimey, sir, they're firing jeeps.'"

Sandy Smith's platoon brought in two prisoners, described by Howard as "miserable little men, in civilian clothes, scantily dressed, very hunry." They were Italians, slave laborers in the Todt Organization. Long, complicated sign-language communication finally revealed that they were the laborers who were designated to put the antiglider poles in place. They had been doing their job, on Wallwork's LZ, when they were rounded up. They appeared quite harmless to Howard.

He gave them some dry biscuits from his forty-eight-hour ration pack, then told Smith to let them loose. The Italians, Howard relates, "immediately went off toward the LZ, where they proceeded in putting up the poles. You can just imagine the laughter that was caused all the way around to see these silly buggers putting up the poles."

More questioning then revealed that the Italians were under the strictest orders from the Todt Organization to have those poles in the ground by twilight, June 6. They were sure the Germans would be back to check on their work, and if it were not done, "they were in for the bloody high jump, so they'd better get on with it, and surrounded by our laughter, they got on with it, putting in the poles."

At about 0800, Spitfires flew over, very high, at six thousand or seven thousand feet. Howard put out a ground-to-air signal, using purposely made signs spread over the ground that meant, "We're in charge here and everything's all right." Three Spitfires—like every other airship, including the gliders, that participated in the invasion, wearing three white bars on each wing—peeled off, dove to one thousand feet, and circled the bridges, doing victory roll after victory roll.

As they pulled away, one of them dropped an object. Howard thought the pilot had jettisoned his reserve petrol tank, but he sent a reconnaissance patrol to find out what it was. The patrol came back, "and to our great surprise and amusement, it was the early editions from Fleet Street. There was a scramble for them amongst all the troops, especially for the *Daily Mirror*, which had a cartoon strip called *Jane*, and they were all scuffling for *Jane*. There were one or two moans about there being no mention of the invasion or of D Company at all."

Throughout the morning, all movement in D Company's area was done crouched over, at a full sprint. Then, shortly after 0900, Howard "had the wonderful sight of three tall figures walking down the road. Now, between the bridges you were generally out of line of snipers, because of the trees along the east side of the canal, and these three tall figures came marching down very smartly, and they turned out to be General Gale, about six feet five inches, flanked by two six-foot brigadiers, Kindersley on one side, our own Air Landing Brigade commander, and Nigel Poett, commanding the 5th Para Brigade, on the other. And it really was a wonderful sight because they were turned out very, very smartly, wearing berets and in battle dress, and marching in step down the road. It was a pure inspiration to all my chaps seeing them coming down." Richard Todd said that "for sheer bravado and bravery it was one of the most memorable sights I've ever seen."

Gale had come down by glider, about 0300, and established his headquarters in Ranville. He and his brigadiers were on their way to consult with Pine Coffin, whose 7th Battalion was hotly engaged with enemy patrols in Bénouville and Le Port. Gale called out to D Company, as he marched along, "Good show, chaps." After a briefing from Howard, Gale and his companions marched across the bridge. They were shot at, but were not hit, and never flinched.

As they disappeared into Pine Coffin's headquarters,

two gunboats suddenly appeared, coming up from the coast headed toward Caen. They were coming from the small harbor in Ouistreham, which was under attack by elements of Lord Lovat's Commando brigade. The gunboats were obviously aware that the bridge was in unfriendly hands, because the lead boat came on at a steady speed, firing its 20-mm cannon at the bridge. Parr could not shoot back with the antitank gun because the bridge and its superstructure blocked his field of fire. Corporal Godbolt, commanding #2 platoon, was on the bank with a Piat. Howard ordered his men to hold fire until the first gunboat was in Godbolt's range. Then some of the 7th paras on the other side started firing at the boat, and Godbolt let go, at maximum range, and to his amazement he saw the Piat bomb explode inside the wheelhouse. The gunboat turned sideways, the bow plunged into the para bank, the stern jammed against D Company's side of the canal.

Germans started running off the stern, hands high, shouting, "*Kamerad, Kamerad.*" The captain, dazed but defiant, had to be forced off the boat. Howard remembers him as "an eighteen- or nineteen-year-old Nazi, very tall, spoke good English. He was ranting on in English about what a stupid thing it was for us to think of invading the Continent, and when his Führer got to hear about it that we would be driven back into the sea, and making the most insulting remarks, and I had the greatest difficulty stopping my chaps from getting hold and lynching that bastard on the spot." But Howard knew that intelligence would want to see the officer immediately, so he had the prisoner marched off toward the POW cage in Ranville. "And he had to be gagged and frog-marched because he was so truculent and shouting away all through the time."

The sappers poured over the boat, examining the equipment, looking for ammunition and guns. One of them found a bottle of brandy and stuck it in his battle smock. His commander, Jock Neilson, noticed the bulge. "Hey, what have you got there?" The sapper showed him the brandy. Neilson straightaway took it, saying, "You are not old enough for that." The sapper complains, "I never saw a drop of that bloody brandy."

D Company had now fired its much-maligned Piat guns twice. One shot had knocked out a tank and sent a second tank scurrying. The second shot had knocked out a gunboat and forced a second one to turn tail and run. D Company had now captured two bridges, the ground between them, and one gunboat.

Near Caen, von Luck was close to despair. The naval bombardment raining down on Caen was much the most tremendous he had seen in all his years at war. Although his assembly point was camouflaged and so far untouched, he knew that when he started to move—when he finally got the order to go—he would be spotted immediately by the Allied reconnaissance aircraft overhead, his position reported to the big ships out in the Channel, and a torrent of 12-inch and 16-inch shells would come down on his head.

Under the circumstances, he doubted that he could get through the 6th Airborne and recapture the bridges. His superiors agreed with him, and they decided that they would destroy the bridges and thus isolate the 6th Airborne. They began to organize a gunboat packed with infantry, meanwhile sending out frogmen and a fighter-bomber from Caen to destroy the bridges.

At about 1000, the German fighter-bomber came flying directly out of the sun, over the river bridge, skimming along just above the trees lining the road, obviously headed for the canal bridge. Howard dived into his pillbox; his men dived into trenches. They poked their heads out to watch as the pilot dropped his bomb. It was a direct hit on the bridge tower. But it did not explode. Instead, it clanged onto the bridge and then dropped into the canal. It was a dud.

The dent is there on the bridge to this day. Howard's comment is "What a bit of luck that was," which says the least of it. Howard adds, with professional approval, "And what a wonderful shot it was by that German pilot."

The two frogmen were, in the daylight, easily disposed of by riflemen along the banks of the canal. On the ground, however, the Germans were pushing the British back. Nigel Taylor's was the only company of 7th Battalion in Bénouville. It ws desperately understrength and very hard pressed by the increasingly powerful German counterattacks. The two companies in Le Port were similarly situated, and like Taylor were having to give up some ground.

As the Germans moved forward, they began putting some of their SPVs into action. These vehicles belonged to von Luck's regiment but were attached to forward companies that were expected to act on their own initiative rather than report back to the regimental assembly area. The British called the rocket launchers on the SPVs "Moaning Minnies." "The thing we most remember about them," Howard says, "apart from the frightful noise, which automatically made you dive for cover, but the thing we most noticed was the tremendous accuracy."

Between explosions, Wally Parr dashed across the road to see Howard. "I got a feeling," he panted, "that there is somebody up there on that water tower spotting for the Minnies." He explained that the water tower, located near the maternity hospital, had a ladder up to the top, and that he could see something up there. Wouldn't Howard please give him permission to have a go at it? Howard agreed. "And you couldn't see Wally's arse for dust," he recalls, as Parr dashed back across the road to his gun.

Parr bellowed out, "NUMBER-ONE GUN!" As he did so, there was one of those strange lulls that occur in so many battles. In the silence Parr's great Cockney voice carried across the battlefield, from Le Port to Bénouville, from the canal to the river. Now, as Howard points out, there was only one gun; as Parr rejoins, it was the only gun in the entire 6th Airborne Division at that moment, so it really was the number-one gun. Parr then put his crew through a drill that constituted a proper artilleryman's fire order. "Seven hundred, one round. Right five degrees," and so on, all orders preceded by "NUMBER-ONE GUN." Finally, "PREPARE TO FIRE." All around him, the warriors—German as well as British—were fascinated spectators. "FIRE!"

The gun roared, the shell hurtled off. It hit the water tower head on. Great cheers went up all around, berets were tossed into the air, men shook hands joyfully. The only trouble was, the ammunition was armor-piercing.

The shell went in one side and came out the other, without exploding. Streams of water began running out the holes, but the structure was still solid. Parr blasted away again, and again, until he had the tower spurting water in every direction. Howard finally ordered him to quit.

When Gale, Kindersley, and Poett returned from their conference with Pine Coffin, they told Howard that one of his platoons would have to move up into Bénouville and take a position in the line beside Taylor's company. Howard chose #1 platoon. He also sent Sweeney and Fox with their platoons over to the west side, to take a position across from the Gondrée café, where they should hold themselves ready to counterattack in the event of a German breakthrough. "And we thought," Sweeney says, "that this was a little bit unfair. We'd had our battle throughout the night; the Seventh Battalion had come in and taken over the position and we rather felt that we should be left alone for a little bit and that the Seventh should not be calling on our platoons to come help it out."

Sweeney and Fox settled down by a hedge. Back at Tarrent Rushton, a week earlier, Sweeney and Richard Todd had met, because of a confusion in their names—in the British Army all Sweeneys were nicknamed "Todd," and all Todds were known as "Sweeney," after the famous barber in London, Sweeney Todd. On the occasion of their meeting, Sweeney and Todd laughed about the coincidence. Todd's parting words had been, "See you on D-Day." On the outskirts of Le Port, at 1100 hours on D-Day, as Sweeney rested against the hedge, "a face appeared through the bushes and Richard Todd said to me, 'I said I'd see you on D-Day' and disappeared again."

Over in Bénouville, #1 platoon was hotly engaged in street fighting. The platoon had gone through endless hours of practice in street fighting, in London, Southampton, and elsewhere, and had gained experience during the night, at the fighting around the café. Now it gave Taylor's company a much-needed boost as it started driving Germans out of buildings they had recaptured.

Sergeant Joe Kane was in command. "He was a phlegmatic sort of a character," Bailey remembers, "nothing seemed to perturb him." They saw an outhouse in a small field. "Cover me," Kane said to Bailey. "Keep me covered. I'm going to take a crap."

He dashed off to the outhouse. A minute later he dashed back. "I can't face that," Kane confessed. There was no hole in the ground, only a bucket, and nothing to sit on. The bucket looked as if it had not been emptied in days. It was overflowing. "I can't face that," Kane repeated.

Thirty-four years later, Bailey induced Kane to return to Normandy. Bailey had been back often through the years, but this was Kane's initial visit since the war. The first thing Kane wanted to do was to go to that outhouse to see if the bucket had been emptied out yet. But it was gone.

By about midday, most of the 7th Battalion had reported in for duty, some coming singly, some in small groups.

Enough arrived so that Pine Coffin could release Howard's platoons. Howard brought them back to the area between the bridges. The snipers remained active, sporadically the Moaning Minnies continued to come in, battles were raging in Bénouville, Le Port, and to the east of Ranville. D Company was shooting back at the snipers, but as Billy Gray confesses, "We couldn't see them, we were just guessing."

But limited though 7th Para and D Company's control was, they held the bridges.

8

D-DAY: 1200 TO 2400 HOURS

AT NOON, SERGEANT Thornton was sitting in a trench, not feeling so good. He was terribly tired, of course, but what really bothered him was the situation. "You see we were stuck there from twenty past twelve the night before, and the longer we were there, the more stuff was coming over from Jerry, and we were surrounded in a small sort of circle and things were getting bloody hot, and the longer you sit anywhere, the more you start thinking. Some of them blokes were saying, 'Oh, I don't suppose I'll ever see the skies over England again,' or the skies over Scotland or the skies over Wales or the skies over Ireland." Wally Parr recalls, "The day went on very, very, very wearing. All the time you could feel movement out there and closer contact coming."

In Bénouville and Le Port, 7th Battalion was holding its ground, but just barely. Major Taylor had survived the fire fights of the night. He had also survived, shortly after dawn, the sight of a half-dozen whores, shouting and waving and blowing kisses at his troops from the window of the room Private Bonck had vacated six hours earlier. By midday, the action had hotted up considerably, and Taylor not only had infantry and SPVs to deal with, but tanks.

"As the first tank crept around the corner," Taylor remembers, "I said to my Piat man, 'Wait, wait.' Then, when it was about forty yards away, 'Fire!' And he pulled the trigger, there was just a click, and he turned around and looked at me and said, 'It's bent, sir.'"

A corporal, seeing the situation, leaped out of his slit trench and charged the tank, firing from the hip with his Sten. When he got to the tank, he slapped a Gammon bomb on it and ran off. The tank blew up, slithered across the road, and blocked that road.

Taylor, by this point, had a slashing, open splinter wound in his thigh. He managed to get up to a second-floor window, from which spot he continued to direct the battle. At one stage, Richard Todd recalls, "we could hear Nigel's voice encouraging the chaps. Leg practically blown off and lying up in the window of a house still encouraging the chaps." Nobody had any communications, the radios and field telephones having been lost on the drop. Taylor sent a runner over to Pine Coffin to report that he had only thirty men left, most of them wounded, and asking whether anything could be done to help. That was when Pine Coffin told Howard to send a D Company platoon into Bénouville.

There had as yet been no determined German armored attacks—von Luck was still waiting for orders in his assembly area—which was fortunate for the paratroopers, as they had only Piats and Gammon bombs with which to fight tanks. But panzers could be expected at any time, coming down from Caen into Bénouville, or up from the coast into Le Port.

The panzers had their own problems. Shortly after noon, von Luck was unleashed. Exactly as he had feared, his columns were immediately spotted, and immediately shelled. Over the course of the next couple of hours, his regiment was badly battered. On the west side of the Orne waterways, the other regiment of 21st Panzer Division also rolled into action, one part of it almost reaching Sword Beach, while one battalion moved off to attack Bénouville.

In Le Port, Todd was trying to dislodge a sniper from the church tower. There was open ground around the church, Todd says, "so there was no way of rushing it, and anyway we had very few chaps on the ground at this time. So Corporal Killean, a young Irishman, volunteered to have a go and see if he could get there with his Piat. And he mouseholed through some cottages, going inside them and knocking holes through from one to the other so he was able to get to the end cottage. He ran out and got his Piat under a hedge and he let fly a bomb, and he hit a hole right where he wanted to in the church tower. He let off two more. And after a while he reckoned that he had indeed killed the sniper."

Killean dashed to the church. But before entering, he took off his helmet and he said, "I'm sorry to see what I have done to a wee house of God," and crossed himself.

Major Taylor kept glancing at his watch. Relief was supposed to arrive from the beaches, in the form of the

Commandos, by noon. It was 1300 already, and no Commandos. "It was a very long wait," Taylor recalls. "I know the longest day and all that stuff, but this really was a hell of a long day." At his CP, which he had moved into the machine-gun pillbox after getting Bailey to clean up the mess he had made, Howard too kept checking the time, and wondering where the Commandos were.

In Oxford, Joy Howard was up shortly after dawn. She was so busy feeding and bathing and pottying the little ones that she did not turn on the radio. About 10 A.M. her neighbors, the Johnsons, knocked and told her that the invasion had started. "We know Major Howard will be in it somewhere," they said, and insisted that Joy and the children join them for a celebration lunch. They lifted the baby chairs over the fence, and treated Joy to a brace of pheasants, a gift from friends in the country, and a bottle of vintage wine they had been saving for just this occasion.

Joy kept thinking of John's last words, that when she heard the invasion had started she would know that his job was done. They hardly gave her any comfort now, because she realized that for all she knew she was already a widow. As best she could, she put such thoughts out of her mind, and enjoyed the lunch. She spent the afternoon at her household tasks, but with her attention concentrated on the radio. She never heard John's name mentioned, but she did hear of the parachute drops on the eastern flank, and assumed John must be part of that.

Von Luck's panzers were rolling now, or rather moving forward as best they could through the exploding naval shells and the RAF strafing. Major Becker, the genius with vehicles who had built the outstanding SPV capability in von Luck's 125th Regiment, led the battle group descending on Bénouville. He had his Moaning Minnies firing as fast as he could reload them.

By 1300 the men at the bridge, and those in Bénouville and Le Port, were beginning to feel disconcertingly like the settlers in the circled-up wagon train, Indians whooping all around them as they prayed for the cavalry to show up. They had sufficient ammunition to throw back probing attacks, but could not withstand an all-out assault, not alone anyway.

Tod Sweeney was gloomily considering the situation, sitting next to Fox. Suddenly he nudged Fox. "Listen," he said. "You know, Dennis, I can hear bagpipes."

Fox scoffed at this. "Oh, don't be stupid, Tod, we're in the middle of France; you can't hear bagpipes."

Sergeant Thornton, in his trench, told his men to listen, that he heard bagpipes. "Go on," they replied, "what are you talking about? You must be bloody nuts." Thornton insisted that they listen.

Howard, at his CP, was listening intently. Back at Tarrent Rushton, he, Pine Coffin, and the commander of the Commandos, the legendary Lord Lovat, had arranged for recognition signals when they met in Normandy. Lovat, arriving by sea, would blow his bagpipes when he approached the bridge, to indicate that he was coming. Pine Coffin's bugler would blow back, with one call meaning the road in was clear, another that it was contested.

The sound of the bagpipe became unmistakable; Pine Coffin's bugler answered with a call that meant there was a fight going on around the bridges.

Lovat's piper, Bill Millin, came into view, then Lovat. It was a sight never to be forgotten. Millin was beside Lovat, carrying his great huge bagpipe, wearing his beret. Lovat had on his green beret, and a white sweater, and carried a walking stick, "and he strode along," Howard remembers, "as if he were on exercise back in Scotland."

The Commandos came on, a Churchill tank with them. Contact had been made with the beachhead. To the men of D Company, it was the arrival of the cavalry. "Everybody threw their rifles down," Sergeant Thornton reminisces, "and kissed and hugged each other, and I saw men with tears rolling down their cheeks. I did honestly. Probably I was the same. Oh, dear, celebrations I shall never forget."

When Georges Gondrée saw Lovat coming, he got a tray, a couple of glasses, and a bottle of champagne, then went dashing out of his café, shouting and crying. He caught up to Lovat, who was nearly across the bridge, and with a grand gesture offered him champagne. Lovat gave a simple gesture of "No, thanks," in return, and marched on.

The sight was too much for Wally Parr. He ran out to Gondrée, nodding his head vigorously and saying, "*Oui, oui, oui.*" Gondrée, delighted, poured. "Oh, dear," Parr says, remembering the occasion, "that was good champagne."

Lovat met Howard at the east end of the bridge, piper Millin just behind him. "John," Lovat said as they shook hands, "today history is being made." Howard briefed him on the situation, telling Lovat that once he got his troops over the bridge, it was clear sailing. But, Howard warned, be careful going over the bridge. Lovat nevertheless tried to march his men across. As a consequence, he had nearly a dozen casualties. Doc Vaughan, who treated them, noted that most were shot through their berets, and killed instantly. Commandos coming later started putting on their helmets to cross the bridge.

The last of the Commandos to pass through handed over to Howard a couple of bewildered-looking German soldiers, wearing only their underwear. They had run for it when D Company stormed the bridge, then had hidden in a hedge along the canal towpath. When they saw the Commandos coming from the coast they decided it was time to give themselves up. The Commando who handed them over to Howard said, with a wide grin, "Here you are, sir, a couple of the Panzoff Division!"

A few of the tanks coming up from the beaches went on into Bénouville, where they set up a solid defensive line. Most crossed the bridge to go to Ranville and the east, to bolster the 6th Airborne Division in its fight against the 21st Panzer Division.

The Germans tried a counterattack, coming straight up the canal. At about 1500 hours, a gunboat came from Caen, loaded with troops. Bailey saw it first and alerted Parr, Gray, and Gardner. They had a heated discussion about range. When they fired, they were thirty yards short. The boat started to turn. When it was about halfway round, they fired again, and hit the stern. The boat chugged off, back toward Caen, trailing smoke.

From about midafternoon onward, the situation around the bridge stabilized. The 8th Heavy Grenadiers and Major Becker's battle group had fought bitterly. But, as

Kortenhaus admits, "We failed because of heavy resistance. We lost thirteen tanks [out of seventeen]." The Germans continued sniping and shooting the Moaning Minnies, but they were no longer attacking in any strength.

"It was a beautiful evening," Nigel Taylor remembers. Along about 1800 hours, when he was sure his position in Bénouville was secure, he had himself carried down to the Gondrée café, so that he could be tended to at the aid post. When his leg wounds were bandaged, he hobbled outside and sat at a table just beyond the front door. "And Georges Gondrée brought me a glass of champagne, which was very welcome indeed after that sort of day, I can tell you. And then that evening, just before it got dark, there was a tremendous flight of aircraft, British aircraft, came in and they did a glider drop and a supply drop on our side of the canal. It was a marvelous sight, it really was. All this time hundreds of gliders, hundreds of the damned things, and of course they were also dropping supplies on chutes out of their bomb doors. All this stuff coming down, and then it seemed only a very few minutes afterward, there were all these chaps in jeeps, towing antitank guns and God knows what, coming down the road through Le Port, and over this bridge."

Taylor sipped his champagne and felt good. "And at that moment I can remember thinking to myself, 'My God, we've done it!'"

Among the gliders were the men of Brigadier Kindersley's Air Landing Brigade, D Company's parent outfit. The companies, with their heavy equipment, began moving across the bridge, toward Ranville and beyond to Escoville, which they were scheduled to attack that night or the following morning. As the Ox and Bucks marched past, Parr, Gray, and the others called out, "Where the hell you been?" and "War's over," and "A bit late for parade, chaps," and other such nonsense.

Howard's orders were to hand over to a seaborne battalion when it came up, then join the Ox and Bucks in or near Escoville. About midnight, the Warwickshire Regiment arrived. Howard briefed the commander. Parr handed over his antitank gun to a sergeant, showing him how to work it ("I was a real expert on German artillery by this time," Parr says. "I was the cat's whiskers, wasn't I?").

Howard told his men to load up. Someone found a horse cart—but no horse. The cart was a big, cumbersome thing, but the men had a lot to carry. All their own equipment, plus the German gear they had picked up (every soldier who could had abandoned his Enfield for a Schmeisser, or his Bren for an MG 34), filled the cart.

D Company started off, headed east, toward the river bridge and over it to Ranville. Howard was no longer under the command of Pine Coffin and Poett; he reverted to his regular chain of command and hereafter reported to his battalion colonel, Mike Roberts. He had carried out his orders, and almost exactly twenty-four hours after his men stormed the bridge, he handed over his objectives intact and secure.

Jack Bailey found it hard to leave. "You see," he explains, "we had been there a full day and night. We rather felt that this was our bit of territory."

9

D-DAY PLUS ONE TO D-DAY PLUS NINETY

BÉNOUVILLE WAS AS far inland as the British seaborne units got on D-Day. Not until August did they penetrate through Caen and beyond. The original plan had been to drive the armor coming in over the beaches right through Bénouville, along the canal road, straight into Caen. But the fierceness of the opposition at Bénouville and Le Port and Ranville convinced the British high command that prudence required going over to the defensive. So, after spending June 6 on bold and aggressive offensive operations, the British spent June 7 to nearly the end of August on the defensive, attempting only once—in mid-July, in operation Goodwood—to break out.

D Company's role in this defensive phase of the battle was unspectacular, with none of the glamour, excitement, or satisfaction that was inherent in the coup de main operation, but with far higher casualties. D Company, in short, became an ordinary infantry company.

The process began just after midnight in the first minutes of June 7. The company marched away from the bridges, pulling the cart loaded with the implements of war behind it. "But that blasted farm cart," Tod Sweeney remembers, "was always running off the road." It was a narrow, poorly graded road, lots of trees running along it, pitch-black. Jack Bailey says, "I reckoned you needed two ox on this cart, because no matter how you pulled it, it kept running off the road."

The swearing, Bailey says, was the most spectacular he ever heard (and he became a regimental sergeant major in the postwar Army, so he heard a lot). Howard tried in vain to get the men to keep quiet.

Eventually, D Company gave up on the cart. Long marches under heavy packs when already exhausted were second nature to D Company. Every man shouldered what he could, some of the equipment was left behind in the hated cart, and off D Company marched, like infantrymen from time out of mind, staggering under the weight of the load.

It was a depleted D Company that marched along toward Ranville. Howard had landed in Normandy twenty-four hours earlier with 181 officers and men. His battle casualties, considering that he had been in continuous action, were remarkably small—two men killed and fourteen wounded. One platoon remained unaccounted for.

His administrative losses had been heavy. After unloading their gliders, and after the Commandos had opened a road, the glider pilots were under orders to go down to the beaches and use their special orders from Montgomery to get themselves back to England.

In the afternoon, the pilots had done as ordered, depriving Howard of another ten men.* As communications improved between Bénouville and the coast, his sappers were taken from him, to rejoin their parent units. That cost almost two dozen men. And as soon as the march ended, he would have to turn over Fox's and Smith's platoons to B Company—another forty men gone. His reinforced company in the early hours of June 6 had numbered 181; in the early hours of June 7 it numbered 76. And when Fox and Smith returned to B Company, Howard's only officer fit for duty was Sweeney. All the others were either dead, wounded, or missing.

D Company marched around Ranville. It was dark, there were numerous bends in the roads and a profusion of crossroads, and paratroopers scurrying in every direction. D Company got lost. Howard called for a break, then talked to Sweeney. "I'm not very happy about this, Tod. We should have met the regiment by this time, because their tail should be about here, so I don't want to take the company down the road. Will you go ahead with a couple of chaps and see if you can make contact with the regiment, then come back here and meet me?"

Sweeney set off with Corporal Porter and one private. "We came to Herouvillette," Sweeney reports, "and it was a very eerie place, there were pigeons going in and out and making pigeon noises, there were parachutists

* At the beach, Oliver Boland was interviewed by a newspaper reporter. He gave a brief account of what happened at the canal bridge. The following day, *The Times* carried an article on the coup de main, giving D Company its first publicity. There would be a great deal to follow.

still dangling from buildings, dead bodies." Sweeney was supposed to turn in Herouvillette in the direction of Escoville, but he missed the turn, wandered about for an hour, finally found the right road, and set off for Escoville and the regiment.

One hundred yards down the road, he saw a dark shape ahead. Motioning for a quiet, careful advance, he moved toward it. There was a clang of a steel door, indicating a German armored vehicle ahead. Sweeney and his men had practiced for exactly this situation during the years at Bulford. Sweeney pulled a grenade, threw it, and started running back toward Herouvillette, while Corporal Porter provided covering fire with his Bren gun.

Sweeney was legging it down the road. "Now the other chap was a big, slow farm lad who couldn't really run at all. He had never done anything athletic and as we were going down the road, he passed me, which I felt very upset about, this chap passing me. I said, 'Here, private, wait for me.' It seemed to me to be quite wrong that he should be racing past me down the road."

The Germans had sprung to life. Tracer bullets were whizzing past Sweeney and the private. Porter kept blazing away with his Bren. Sweeney and the private ducked behind a building to wait for Porter, but the fire fight continued and Sweeney decided he had to report back to Howard, with or without Porter. When Sweeney did report, Howard confessed that as he had listened to the fire fight, his thought had been "My God, there goes the last of my subalterns."

Sweeney said, "John, there is no good going down

there. Wherever the regiment has got to it hasn't gone down the road toward Escoville and I've just run into an armored car and I've lost Corporal Porter." Howard said all right, they would go back the other way and find the regiment. They did, and discovered that they had never been lost, but that the regiment had camped for the night in a different location than Howard had been told. He had marched near it twice in the last two hours. It was 0300 hours.

Howard reported to battalion headquarters. There, to his great delight, he saw Brian Priday and Tony Hooper. After greetings, they told their story—how they realized they were at the wrong bridge, how Hooper had become a prisoner, then was freed as Priday killed his captors with his Sten gun, how they set off cross-country, through swamps and over bogs, hiding in Norman barns, engaging in fire fights with German patrols, joining up with paratroopers, finally making it to Ranville. D Company now had twenty-two more men, and two more officers, including the second-in-command. Howard reorganized the company into three platoons, under the three remaining officers.

By 0400, the platoon commanders had put their men into German bunks, then found beds in a château for themselves. They slept for two hours. At 0600 hours, Howard got them up; the company was then on the road by 0630. When it came to the road junction and the left turn toward Escoville, as Sweeney relates, "There was Corporal Porter sitting on the side of the road with his Bren gun, and he looked at me and said, 'Where did you get to, sir?' I said, 'I'm sorry, Porter, but I really had to get back and report.'"

D Company moved on, toward Escoville. "Suddenly we came under very heavy fire," Howard reports, "mainly from a hull down 88." He took some casualties before setting out cross-country through some trees, coming up to the farm he had picked as his company headquarters. He put his three platoons into position. They immediately came under mortar, SPV, tank, sniper, and artillery fire. They were being attacked by the 2d Panzer Grenadiers of von Luck's 125th Regiment of the 21st Panzer Division. "And these people," Sweeney is frank to say, "were a different kettle of fish from the people we had been fighting at the bridges." Casualties were heavy, but D Company held its position.

About 1100 hours, Howard started to make another round of his platoons. Sweeney's was the first stop. Howard began studying the enemy with his binoculars, "then there was a zip and I was knocked out." There was a hole right through his beret, and enough blood to convince the men that he was mortally wounded.

When that word went around among the men in Sweeney's platoon, their reaction was to start organizing patrols to find and kill the sniper who had shot their major. In relating this incident, Tappenden commented: "Every man in the company admired Major Howard more than almost anyone alive, because he was a man that if he couldn't do it, you couldn't do it, and you weren't asked to do it. We worshipped him and we wanted revenge." Fortunately, Howard regained consciousness within a half hour—he had only been creased—and told the men to hold their positions.

By midafternoon, the Germans had pushed forward their attack, to the point that there were German tanks between Hooper's platoon and the other two. Orders came down from battalion to withdraw to Herouvillette. The retreat was carried out in fairly good order, considering the pressure and considering that Howard had lost nearly half his fighting strength in half a day.

"We got caught up something chronic in Escoville," Parr admits. He and Bailey covered the retreat. When they pulled back behind a château, Parr gasped out to the padre standing there with the wounded, "Let's get going. They are right behind us." The padre replied that he was going to stay with the wounded, be taken prisoner with them, so that he could be with them in their POW camp to offer what help he could. Bailey and Parr looked at each other. Then they organized some of the chaps, found some improvised stretchers, and carried the wounded back to Herouvillette. "It wasn't far," Parr says, "only three-quarters of a mile."

Parr continues: "When we got there, as far as the eye could see, lined up in the ditch, there was the rest of the fellows, all facing the way the Jerries was coming. And the regimental sergeant major, almost with tears in his eyes, right there in front, striding up and down, was saying in a great booming voice, 'Well done, lads. Well done. Wait till the bastards come at us this time. We'll mow 'em down. I'm proud of you. Well done.'"

The men lay there, Parr recalls, some wounded, some shell-shocked, everyone "just thumped to pieces," with their Bren guns and their captured German weapons and their mortars and their Piats, and the sergeant major strode on, "swearing like blue blazes about what we were going to do to the bastards."

It is a scene more reminiscent of World War I than World War II. When the Germans did come, D Company mowed them down as if it were the Battle of Mons all over again. But that only highlighted the transformation that had taken place in D Company's role. On June 6 it had been at the cutting edge of tactical innovation and technological possibilities. On June 7 it was fighting with the same tactics ordinary infantry companies used thirty years earlier, at Mons and throughout World War I.

Howard set up headquarters in Herouvillette. The company stayed there for four days, always under attack by mortar and artillery fire, sometimes having to fight off tanks and infantry. He was down to less than fifty fighting men.

The company moved twice more, then settled down into defensive positions it was to hold for almost two months. "The only thing we could do was to send out fighting patrols every night to bring back prisoners," Howard says. He went out on patrols himself. One night he took Wally Parr along. It was a macabre setting, rather like what Howard imagined Verdun had been. They were in the area where the Battle of Bréville had just been fought. In the moonlight, corpses were scattered about, mainly men of the 51st Highland Division, who had been killed by an artillery concentration. Howard and Parr found one group of six men, sitting in a circle in their trench, playing cards. Though they were still sitting up, holding their cards, and though they had no bullet or shrapnel wounds, they were all dead. They had been killed by concussion.

During this period, Howard says, "The biggest problem I had was keeping up the morale of the troops, because we had always got the impression that we would be withdrawn from Normandy to come back and refit in the U.K. for another airborne operation." After all, the glider pilots had been withdrawn and were already in England preparing for future operations.

There was another morale problem, the constant shelling. "Chaps began to go bomb happy," Howard says. "At first many of us tended to regard it as a form of cowardice and we were highly critical. I remember that I tended to take a very tough and almost unfeeling line about it. But after a time, when we began to see some of our most courageous comrades going under, we soon changed our minds. We could see that it was a real sickness. Men would hide away and go berserk during bombardments, and they became petrified during attacks. They could not be used for patrols, or even sentry duty, and the only answer was to hand them over to the medical officer, who, once he was satisfied it was a genuine case, had the man evacuated as a casualty. It was pathetic to see good men go down."

Howard himself almost went under. By D-Day plus four, he had gone for five days with almost no sleep. In the month prior to D-Day, he had been under the most intense pressure. His losses in Escoville and Herouvillette were heartrending. "I felt terribly depressed and pessimistic," Howard admits, "feeling quite sure that the Allied bridgehead was going to collapse on our vulnerable left flank. However, once the CO and the MO persuaded me what was wrong, with quiet threats of evacuation, I luckily shook myself out of it." Shaking himself from the memory of it, Howard concludes, "It was an awful experience."

From the experience, Howard learned a lesson. He got regular, if short, periods of sleep for himself, and he saw to it that the platoon leaders, "as far as possible, try to arrange for regular stand-down periods for everyone in turn and see that they got their heads down. Especially when they were under attack or shell fire."

Another manifestation of the pressure on D Company was self-inflicted wounds, "shots through the leg or foot," as Howard relates, "usually said to have occurred when cleaning weapons. They were very difficult to prove." Switching to a larger subject, Howard notes that "keeping up morale when casualties are heavy is always a big test of leadership. Good discipline and esprit de corps go a long way toward overcoming it, but I found keeping the men well occupied was as good a cure as any. Active aggressive patrolling, sniping parties, marches behind the line, and, above all, keep everyone in the picture. Glean all you can from HQ by way of information about how the battle is going and have regular meetings with the men to pass it on."

Howard went to HQ not only to find out what was going on, but to do all those little things a good company commander does. Making certain there were plenty of cigarettes, for example ("the rate of smoking among the troops stepped up amazingly," Howard recalls), with an extra supply after a battle or a shelling. Ensuring the prompt arrival and distribution of the mail ("essential for maintaining good morale"). Howard would send runners back to HQ for the mail if he thought he could save a few minutes. Getting fresh bread. (The first shipment did not arrive until D-Day plus twenty-five. "I was astounded over how much we longed for it.")

Cleaning weapons was an obsession. First thing in the morning, after the dawn stand-to and breakfast, everything came out—rifles, machine guns, Piats, mortars, grenades, ammunition—and everything was cleaned, oiled, and inspected. Almost everyone had a Schmeisser by this time.

During this period of near-static warfare, Howard says, "one thing I could never get used to was the smells of battle. Worst of these was dead and putrefying bodies. The men were buried, but there was dead livestock everywhere just rotting away. In the middle of summer it was hell. At the Château Saint Come there was a stable full of wonderful racehorses caught in a burning building. The appalling smell from that place spread over a very wide area; it was so sickening. We eventually dealt with it by loads of lime. You can imagine the swarms and swarms of flies that pyre caused. Then there was the acrid smell of cordite and explosives following every bombardment. It hung about for days.

"It was impossible to get away from all these ghastly smells, and on top of the inevitable discomforts arising from the lack of facilities for washing, one simply longed to be away from it all, where the air was fresh, lovely clean hot water available, endless changes of light clothing, and beds with cool, clean white sheets."

But the biggest morale problem of all was the nagging question, in every man's mind, "Why are we being wasted like this? Surely there must be other bridges between here and Berlin that will have to be captured intact."

* * *

It is indeed a mystery why the War Office squandered D Company. It was an asset of priceless value, a unique company in the whole British Army. Huge sums had been spent on its training. Its combination of training and skills and handpicked officers was unsurpassed. It could leap into action from a glider crash in a matter of seconds; it could move out and do its tasks without being told, and with the precision of a well-coached football team. It could kill. It could fight tanks with hand-held weapons. It had endurance. It had dash. It liked fighting at night. Its accomplishments had been recognized. On July 16, in a field in Normandy, Field Marshal Montgomery personally awarded John Howard a DSO.

Despite all this, the War Office allowed D Company to bleed nearly to death in front of the German guns, and without giving the company proper weapons for fighting a panzer regiment. Sweeney was wounded, Priday was wounded, Hooper was wounded—by August none of D Company's original officers were left, save Howard himself. All the sergeants were gone. Thornton had a leg wound and had been evacuated; so had Corporal Parr.

On D-Day plus eleven, Howard was wounded again. A mortar hit a tree, a piece of shrapnel hit some grenades in the trench, they exploded, and Howard got shrapnel in his back. His driver took him back to an aid post. A surgeon removed the shrapnel. When he finished, the doctor told Howard to lie there for a while. Enemy mortar shells started dropping, and everybody ran for cover. Howard looked around. He was alone in the operating room. He jumped off the table, put his shirt and battle smock on, and went out into the driveway, where he saw his driver taking shelter under the jeep. "Let's get back to the company," Howard told him. "It's quieter there than it is here."

Howard had returned to the front lines, but all the documentation at the aid post showed that he had been evacuated to England. As a consequence, his mail was diverted to a hospital there. He had been getting daily letters from Joy, but they suddenly stopped coming. The V-1s and V-2s were raining down on England at that time, and he tortured himself with thoughts of her death and the loss of his children. That experience, Howard says, "nearly sent me round the bend."

It was worse for Joy. She got a telegram from the War Office. It was supposed to read, "Your husband has suffered a mortar wound and is in hospital." In fact, it read, "Your husband has suffered a mortal wound and is in hospital." The War Office told a frantic Joy that he was in such-and-such hospital. She called there and was told he never arrived. No one knew where he was. For two weeks John and Joy suffered, before the matter was worked out.

Sergeant Heinz Hickman was fighting across from D Company once again. He gives a description of what it was like from the German point of view: "There was man-to-man fighting, fighting in the rubble along the streets. You didn't know who was running in front of you and who was running behind you; you couldn't recognize anything and everybody ran. In the daytime we took position, and nighttime we moved either to the left, to the right, back. I had a map case in my belt.

The map made no difference to me because I didn't know where I was. So you were moved two kilometers to the left, two kilometers to the right, three kilometers forward, or back again. And it stank, and there was the smoke, everywhere, all the time. Every day you counted your men; one section had two men left, another three. I was a platoon commander with five men left to command."

On September 2, while trying to swim the Orne River, Hickman was wounded, captured, interrogated, and sent on to a POW camp in England.

Von Luck was also having a bad time. Every two or three days, he would launch armored attacks. But every time his tanks moved, observers in balloons would spot him, radio to the big ships off shore and the planes overhead, and "Whomp," down on his tanks would come naval gunfire and strafing Spitfires.

On July 18, there was the biggest bombardment von Luck ever experienced, from bombers, naval warships, and artillery. Monty was launching operation Goodwood, designed to break through the German lines, capture Caen, and drive on toward Paris. As the barrage moved past him, von Luck set out for the front on his motorcycle. He arrived at a battery of 88-mms, pointing skyward, still smoking, commanded by a Luftwaffe major. Off to his right, less than a kilometer away, von Luck could see twenty-five British tanks of the Guards Armored Division moving forward. He pointed them out to the battery commander and said, "Major, depress your guns and kill those tanks." The major refused. He said he was a Luftwaffe officer, not responsible to the

Wehrmacht, and his target was bombers, not tanks. Von Luck repeated his order. Same response.

Von Luck pulled his pistol, pointed it between the major's eyes at a six-inch range, and said, "Major, in one minute you are either a dead man or you will have won a medal." The major depressed his four guns, started shooting, and within minutes had crippled twenty-five British tanks. Shortly thereafter, Monty called off operation Goodwood.

In late August, 21st Panzer Division was pulled out of the Normandy battle. Von Luck and his men were sent over to the Rhone Valley to meet the threat of the invading forces in southern France. Privates Romer and Bonck were POWs.

In early September, the British broke through. The Germans were on the run, the British hot after them. D Company was part of the pursuit. It reached a village near the Seine. Howard established his headquarters in a school. The schoolmaster came to see him. The Frenchman said he wanted to show some appreciation for being liberated. "But I've got nothing of any value that I can give you," he confessed to Howard. "The Germans took everything of value before they left, in prams and God knows what, but the one thing I can give you is my daughter."

And he brought his eighteen-year-old daughter from behind his back, and offered her to Howard. "It was so pathetic," Howard remembers. Making the scene even sadder, Howard believes that after he declined, the schoolmaster passed his daughter on down to the enlisted men, who accepted the gift.

The following day, on the Seine itself, Howard came into a village, "and that's where we saw all these girls with all their hair cut off and tied to a lamppost and everything, gruesome sight really." He wondered if that kind of humiliation was being handed out to those friendly little whores back in Bénouville, who had been as eager to please the British troops as they had the Germans. Or to the young mothers in the maternity hospital. Whose babies could those be, anyway, with all able-bodied Frenchmen off in slave labor or POW camps?

Howard thought it a bit unfair of the French to take out all their frustrations on one single element of the whole society. Almost everyone in France had got through the German occupation by doing whatever it was that he or she did, quietly and without a fuss. One of the things young girls do is to establish romantic attachments with young boys. There were only young German boys around, no French. The girls had no choice, but to Howard's dismay they had to bear the brunt of the first release of pent-up outrage following the liberation celebration. Those Frenchmen with guilty consciences did most of the haircutting.

On September 5, after ninety-one days of continuous combat, D Company was withdrawn from the lines. It traveled by truck to Arromanches, was driven out to Mulberry Harbor, climbed up scrambling decks, and set sail for Portsmouth. Then by train to Bulford, where the members of the company moved back into their old rooms and took stock of their losses. Howard was the only officer of the original coup de main party still with them. All the sergeants and most of the corporals were gone. All told, D Company had fallen from its D-Day strength of 181 down to 40.

10

D-DAY PLUS THREE MONTHS TO D-DAY PLUS FIFTY YEARS

AFTER ONE NIGHT at Bulford, the company went on leave. Howard drove up to Oxford, for a joyful reunion and a glorious rest. On the morning of September 17, he relates, "I got up and saw all these planes milling around with gliders on them, and of course I knew that something was on." The planes were headed for Arnhem. Howard knew that Jim Wallwork and the other pilots were up there, "and I silently wished old Jim good luck."

Howard did not know it, but Sergeant Thornton was also up there, with a group of paratroopers. When Thornton was evacuated from Normandy, he had a quick recovery from his wound. Then, rather than wait for D Company to return, he had transferred to the 1st Airborne Division, gone through his jump training, and was going in with Colonel John Frost's 2d Battalion. Thornton fought beside Frost at Arnhem Bridge for four days, and was captured with him. When I suggested to him that he probably was the only man to have been at both famous bridges, he modestly and typically denied it, saying there must have been others.

Howard could hardly imagine such a thing, but none of those gliders overhead carried coup de main parties, not for the bridge at Arnhem, nor the one at Nijmegen. It seems possible that had D Company been available, someone would have thought to lay on coup de main parties for the bridges. Speculation on what Howard's company, flown in by Wallwork, Ainsworth, Boland, and the other pilots, might have accomplished at Arnhem and Nijmegen makes for one of the more tantalizing "what ifs" of World War II. If the bridge at Nijmegen had been captured by a coup de main, the American paratroopers would not have had to fight a desperate battle to take it. Rather, they could have set up a defensive perimeter, with the strength to spare to send men over to Arnhem to help out. At Arnhem, with glider help, Frost could have held both ends of his bridge, greatly simplifying his problems.

But it was not to be. D Company had not been pulled out of Normandy until it was an exhausted, battered remnant of its old self, and evidently no other company could take its place. Certainly there were no coup de main parties in the gliders over Howard's head. He watched them straighten out and then head east, and he again wished them good luck.

In late September 1944, ten days after Arnhem, Howard reported back to Bulford. He set out to rebuild D Company. Reinforcements brought it up to full strength; Howard's job was to make the recruits into genuine airborne soldiers. He started with basics—physical and weapon training. By mid-November, he was ready to take the recruits on street-fighting exercises, to get his men accustomed to live ammunition. He selected an area of Birmingham, arranged for bunks for the men, and returned to Bulford.

On Monday, November 13, Howard decided to spend the night with Joy, as Oxford was on the route to Birmingham. He brought two Oxford residents with him, Corporal Stock and his new second-in-command, Captain Osborne. Although Stock was his driver, Howard insisted on taking the wheel, because Stock did not drive fast enough to suit him.

About half-past five, just as it was getting dusk, on a narrow, twisting road, they met a Yank convoy of six-ton trucks. They were on a right-hand bend. Suddenly, with no warning, Howard "saw this six-ton truck in front of me. He'd lost his place in the convoy and he was obviously leapfrogging up, and it was all over so quickly."

They had a head-on crash. Howard was thrown clear, but both legs, his right hip, and his left knee were smashed up. Stock and Osborne escaped with lesser injuries.

Howard was taken to a hospital in Tidworth, where he was on the critical list for three weeks. Joy made the long journey daily to visit. In December, using his connections with the Oxford police, Howard got himself moved to a hospital in Oxford. He remained there until March 1945.

D Company went on to fight in the Battle of the Bulge, then to lead the way on the Rhine crossing, and participate in the drive to the Baltic. The glider pilots were at Arnhem, then flew again in the Rhine crossing.

When Howard came out of the hospital, he was using crutches. By the time his convalescent leave was over, so was the war in Europe. But when he reported for duty, he learned that the Ox and Bucks was going to the Far East, for another glider operation. The battalion commander asked Howard if he could get fit in time. It seemed the authorities wanted to promote him and make him second-in-command of the battalion.

Howard immediately started a running program on a track near his home. On the second day of trying to run laps, his right hip went out of joint, his right leg went dead. He had not allowed his injuries to heal properly, and the strain on the hip from the running caused it to jam, which deadened the nerves running down the leg. Howard went back into the hospital for further operations. When he got out this time, the war in Asia was over.

He wanted to stay in the Army, make a career of it, "but before I knew where I was I was kicked out of the Army, invalided out. My feet just didn't touch."

Howard went into the Civil Service, first on the National Savings Committee, then with the Ministry of Food. In 1946, he had an audience with the King in Buckingham Palace. On June 6, 1954, the tenth anniversary of D-Day, he received a Croix de Guerre *avec Palme* from the French government, which had already renamed the canal bridge, calling it Pegasus Bridge. Later the road that crosses the bridge was named Esplanade Major John Howard.

Howard served as a consultant for Darryl Zanuck in the making of the film *The Longest Day*. Howard, played by Richard Todd, had a prominent role in the film, which of course delighted him. He was less happy about Zanuck's penchant for putting drama ahead of accuracy. Zanuck insisted that there *had* to be explosives in place under the bridge. Zanuck, not Howard, prevailed at the bridge on this occasion—in the film, the sappers are seen pulling out explosives from under the bridge and throwing them into the canal.

In 1974, Howard retired. He and Joy live in a small but comfortable home in the tiny village of Burcot, about six miles from Oxford. Terry and Penny live close enough for the grandchildren to pay regular visits. As old-age pensioners, the Howards do not travel much, but John manages to return to Pegasus Bridge almost every year on June 6. His hip and legs are so mangled that he needs a cane to get around, and then moves only with great pain, but all his enormous energy flows out again when he sees his bridge, and greets Mme. Gondrée, and starts talking to those of his men who made it over for this particular anniversary. Sweeney and Bailey are usually there, and sometimes Wood and Parr and Gray and always some of the others.

Von Luck spent the remainder of the fall of 1944 fighting General Leclerc's French armored division. In mid-December, he was involved in the fighting at the southern end of the Battle of the Bulge. He was surprised at how much the Americans had improved since February 1943, when he had fought them at Kasserine Pass. In the spring of 1945, 21st Panzer went to the Eastern Front, to join in the defense of Berlin. In late April, by then encircled, von Luck was ordered to break a way through the Russian lines, then hold it open so that the Ninth Army could get out and surrender to the Americans. Before attacking the Russians, von Luck called what was left of his regiment together and gave a small talk.

"We are here now," he began, "and I think that it is more or less the end of the world. Please forget about the Thousand-Year Reich. Please forget all about that. You will ask, 'Why then are we going to fight again?' I tell you, there's only one reason you are fighting, it is for your families, your grounds, your homeland. Always think about what will happen when the Russians overcome your wives, your little daughters, your village, our homeland."

The men fought until they were out of ammunition. Von Luck told them, "O.K., now it's finished, everybody is free to go wherever you want." Von Luck himself went to report to the commander of the Ninth Army, and was captured by the Russians. They sent him to a POW camp in the Caucasus, where he spent five years as a coal miner. In 1951 he moved to Hamburg, where he became a highly successful, self-made coffee importer.

Beginning in the mid-1970s, the Swedish military academy has brought von Luck and Howard together to give talks on leadership. They hit it off from the first, and have grown to like each other more with each annual appearance. Today they could only be described as good friends. "So much for war," Howard comments.

Sergeant Heinz Hickman spent the remainder of the war in England as a POW. He liked the country so much that when he was shipped home, he applied for a visa. It was duly granted, and he immigrated to England, got a job, married a British girl, and settled down. One day in the early 1960s one of his friends at work told him that there was a parachute reunion going on that night, and as an old paratrooper himself he might want to attend. Hickman did. There he saw Billy Gray, the same man he had stood opposite at twenty minutes after midnight on June 6, 1944, in front of the café, in the classic stance of legs wide apart, machine gun at the hip, blazing away.

Hickman did not recognize Gray, of course, but during the evening Gray pulled out some photographs of Pegasus Bridge and started to explain the coup de main. Hickman looked at the photos. "I know that bridge," he said. "That's the bridge over the Orne Canal." He and Gray got talking. Later they exchanged visits. A friendship developed. Over the years it grew closer and deeper, until today it can only be described as intimate. They kid each other about what lousy marksmen they were in their youth. "So much for war."

General Sir Nigel Poett, KCB, DSO, had a distinguished military career. Now retired, he lives near Salisbury. Major Nigel Taylor, MC, is a solicitor living near Malvern. Richard Todd continues to pursue his highly successful acting career. (When I interviewed him, he was starring in *The Business of Murder* at the Mayfair.) Major Dennis Fox, MBO, soldiered on for ten years after the war, then became an executive with ITV. Colonel H. J. Sweeney, MC, also stayed in the Army until he was fifty-five; today Tod is the Director General of the Battersea Dog's Home near Old Windsor, and the head of the Ox and Bucks regimental veterans' association.

Major R. A. A. Smith, MC, became a director of both Shell and BP in India; retired today, Sandy lives in Chedworth and runs specialty tours to India. Colonel David Wood, MBE, soldiered on until retirement. He organized staff college visits to Pegasus, where Howard and Taylor would give lectures on what happened. Today David lives in retirement in a country home in Devon.

Staff Sergeant Oliver Boland, DFM, lives in retirement near Stratford-on-Avon. Jack Bailey stayed in the Army, where he became a regimental sergeant major. Today, Jack is head clerk in a London business firm and lives in Catford, near Wally Parr. Dr John Vaughan is in practice in Devon.

Staff Sergeant Jim Wallwork, DFM, worked as a salesman for the first ten years after the war. In 1956, he immigrated to British Columbia, where today he runs a small livestock farm on the edge of the mountains to the east of Vancouver. From his porch, and from his picture window, Jim has a grand view of a valley dropping away before him. The kind of view a glider pilot gets on his last approach to the LZ.

Corporal Wally Parr wanted to stay in the Army, but with a wife and children, he decided he had to get out. He returned to Catford, where he lives today with Irene. One of his sons is in business with him—he runs a window-cleaning business—and another is a promising musician. He is as irrepressible today as he was forty years ago.

Wagger Thornton lives with his wife in quiet retirement in the south of London. His children are university graduates with advanced degrees and already successful professional careers. They have, in short, taken full advantage of the freedom he helped to preserve when he fired his Piat at 0100 June 6, 1944. (He still curses the weapon as "a load of rubbish.")

To my knowledge, there are no intact, still flying Horsa gliders in existence. Zanuck got the blueprints for the Horsa and built one for *The Longest Day*. The Air Ministry judged that the design was inherently bad, that the craft was not airworthy, and that therefore Zanuck could not have a permit to fly it across the Channel, as he had hoped to do. Zanuck had to dismantle the thing, bring it over by ship, and put it together again in France.

The model of the bridge and surrounding area, the one that Howard and his men studied so intently in Tarrent Rushton, is today in the Airborne Forces Museum at Aldershot.

Bénouville has a few new houses, some development, but basically it stands as it stood on June 6, 1944. So does Ranville, where Den Brotheridge is buried, under a tree, in the British military cemetery.

The Gondrée café remains, changed only by the portraits hanging on the wall—portraits of John Howard and Jim Wallwork and Nigel Taylor and the others who came to liberate France and the Gondrées.

Over the next forty years, Mme. Gondrée presided over her tiny café in a grand fashion. To see her on a June 6, surrounded by her many friends from D Company and from the 7th Battalion, chatting away gaily, remembering the great day however many years ago, was to see a happy woman. Before he died in the late seventies, her husband, Georges, made many close British friends, Howard especially. Jack Bailey went duck hunting with Gondrée each year.

When I interviewed Madame, I asked her to describe life during the occupation. She let loose a torrent of words, paragraphs or incidents separated by hearfelt cries of "*Mon Dieu! Mon Dieu!*" She spat out her hatred of Germans. They had taken all the young men. They took all the best food and drink. They smelled bad. They shot people. Everyone had to work for them. There were arrests for no reason. Because there was a reason to arrest them, the Gondrées lived in dread. The worst was having to serve them food and beer.

Madame, in short, still hated the Germans and would not allow them into her café. When Zanuck was shooting *The Longest Day*, he wanted to have half-dressed German soldiers come leaping out of the windows of the café as D Company charged across the bridge. Madame screamed, she yelled, she ran around waving her arms, crying "*Mon Dieu! Mon Dieu!*," and insisting to Zanuck that she had never, never had Germans sleeping in her house, and that he absolutely must take that scene out of the script. Unlike Howard, Madame had her way with Zanuck. The scene was dropped.

When Howard went to the café in the seventies and early eighties, he sometimes brought Hans von Luck with him. Howard told Madame that von Luck might look suspiciously like a German, but that he was in fact a Swede. In addition to Germans, Madame was also death on the Communists, especially French Communists.

She had daughters and grandchildren and many friends. In short, a full and rich life.

Just prior to the fortieth anniversary celebration, Madame fell ill. She had been so pestered by reporters and television crews in the weeks preceding the ceremonies that she had put a sign on the door of her café, "No reporters, no interviews." She took to her bed.

But she rallied for the ceremonies, and on the anniversary went to the services in the Ranville cemetery, leaning on John Howard's arm, using a cane in her other hand, but holding her head proudly high. She was presented to Prince Charles, who had an animated conversation with her in French. She introduced her daughters, Georgette and Arlette. Then Prince Charles turned to John Howard, exclaiming, "Oh, I know all about you." Howard brought forward some of his pilots, including Wallwork, Boland, and Geoff Barkway of #3 glider. Prince Charles knew all about them, too—they discussed the Horsa glider.

For Madame, who was being called the "Mother of the 6th Airborne Division" by the British Press, the excitement proved to be too much. When the ceremonies were finished, she returned to her café, and her bed.

At midnight, Howard and twenty survivors from D Company met on the bridge—among others, Jack Bailey was there, and Wally Parr, Paddy O'Donnell, Jim Wallwork, David Wood, Oliver Boland, Sandy Smith, John Vaughan, Tod Sweeney, and Wagger Thornton. At past reunions, Madame had brought out champagne at 0016 hours on June 6, but she was unable to make it in 1984. Georgette and Arlette Gondrée, along with Howard's daughter Penny, took her place. The corks popped at exactly 0016. The party lasted until past 0300.

The next morning, the Gondrée girls and Howard

wanted to rush Madame to the hospital, but she refused to go until after Howard and the rest of the British airborne veterans had left Normandy. One hour after John Howard drove off to catch the ferry, on June 8, she consented to enter the hospital. She died there on July 2, 1984.

The canal has been widened by some four or five feet, and the water tower is gone. The château stands intact. The machine-gun pillbox that Jack Bailey knocked out and John Howard used as a CP is still there, forming the foundation of the house lived in by the man who operates the swing bridge. The bunkers are all filled in. The antitank gun and its emplacement, where Wally Parr had so much fun, remains. Three stone markers are placed on the sites where the first three gliders crashed.

11

D-DAY PLUS FORTY YEARS TO D-DAY PLUS FIFTY YEARS

THERE HAD BEEN intense worldwide press publicity on the fortieth anniversary of the capture of Pegasus Bridge. Television cameras, radio reporters, hundreds of French, British, and American visitors were present at the annual Ox and Bucks ceremony paying homage to "fallen comrades." Prior to 1984, the ceremony had been a small private occasion attended only by coup de main veterans and their families, and the Gondrée family who always provided champagne for the toast. Since 1984, the annual occasion has been crowded with people and covered by television lights. John Howard comments, "In many ways, the veterans and Gondrée family now regret the occasion has become a public affair rather than the private one."

In 1986, the area between the gliders' landing zone and the canal was designated "Esplanade Major John Howard." In 1987, the French authorities announced that the Café Gondrée and the house had been officially listed as a *Monument Historique*, as the first house to be liberated in France. That same year, however, word arrived that other French authorities had decided to replace Pegasus Bridge with a newer, larger one. The Port of Caen Authority, it turned out, wanted larger ships to be able to pass up and down the canal to the Port.

When the initial plans became available, it was seen that the new bridge was to be located on the south side of the old one (i.e., nearer the café). Strong objections were raised by British veterans and by the Gondrée daughters.

Major Howard took command. After spraying a red line along where the proposed road would run (only a few meters from the front door of the café), Howard took photos and showed them to the Prefect in Caen. He pointed out that the heavy traffic using the road passing so close to the café would quickly undermine and permanently damage the structure of a *Monument Historique.*

The Prefect called for fresh plans to be drawn up. When they became available, Howard was satisfied to see that the new bridge would be constructed exactly where the old one stood and the new road would be no more than a few centimeters nearer the café. The new bridge would be a lifting bridge, same as the old one. He was also promised that the old one would stay in place until after the fiftieth anniversary of D-Day.

In 1988, Howard received a special medal from a special group. The Normandy Veterans' Association was issuing a serially numbered, limited-edition medal for Veterans of the Normandy Campaign. Howard was told that committees of the Association from all over the country had met and unanimously agreed that the medal numbered "1944" should be presented to him, and the citation on it should read as follows: "The first British Commanding Officer to be engaged in action against the enemy on the mainland of France in the Normandy Invasion."

On the forty-fifth anniversary, the Mayor of Ranville unveiled a plaque to commemorate the capture of the river bridge by two platoons of the coup de main party. The bridge was named "Horsa Bridge." There was a big turnout of Ox and Bucks for the occasion, and despite a cold penetrating rain, a large crowd of visitors.

In 1991, the bridge was again threatened by French bureaucracy. The authorities announced in the press the intention to move Pegasus Bridge to the Peace Museum in Caen. Howard and virtually all other veterans of the 6th Airborne Division raised a storm of protest, which led the French to back down, although possibly only temporarily. Until the spring of 1994, the eventual resting place for Pegasus Bridge will be unknowable—but if Howard and the other British veterans have their way, it will remain in the bridge area.

All of these and other events concerning the bridge are regularly reported on in the British press, along with some of the details of an unhappy squabble between the Gondrée sisters over ownership of the café. There have been some bonuses, thanks to the publicity. For one thing, John Howard receives stacks of mail from admirers. He invariably answers, signing off with his well-known "Ham and Jam. John." He especially enjoys his correspondence with young army officers from around the world.

In the mid-1980s a teenage German student named

Frank Montag read this book and was so taken with the story that he worked the next two years on a model of the action. He consulted with Major Howard and Private Romer frequently to ensure accuracy. In 1988, he presented the completed model to the Airborne Forces Museum at Aldershot, where it is on display today. The model portrays the action a few minutes after the landing, with No. 1 platoon crossing the bridge while grenades exploded in the pillbox. It was a labor of love and is much admired by the airborne veterans.

On June 7, 1986, the German sentry Helmut Romer and his fellow sentry Erwin met John Howard on the bridge. Howard took down their oral history, then wrote it up in the third person. It provides a fascinating point of view on the coup de main operation, as well as some needed corrections concerning the German side of the event as recounted in the first edition of this book.

As Howard got their story, Romer and his friend Private Erwin had been called up in 1943 and became seventeen-year-old soldiers in the *Wehrmacht*. They were posted as sentries on the nights of June 5–6. Their duties were to stop and question anyone wanting to cross, examine papers, and so forth. As there was a curfew at night, they normally had little or nothing to do. "It was not an exciting job," Romer told Howard, "but it was certainly better than fighting in Russia or Italy."

Romer went on to give an eyewitness account of Jim Wallwork's landing, as written by Howard: "They heard a strange 'swishing' noise and suddenly saw a large silent aircraft flying low toward the canal bridge from the south and parallel to the canal and they heard it crash in the small field immediately southwest of the bridge around fifty meters away. They concluded that it must be a crashed bomber and started discussing whether they should investigate or awaken the Sergeant who was sleeping in a bunker by the pillbox."

Howard described how as they debated, "they were suddenly confronted by a bunch of wild men numbering ten or more who were charging toward them, guns and rifles at the hips. They were black-faced and wearing camouflaged uniforms and obviously looking for trouble, but strangely they were not firing their weapons."

Romer and Erwin started to run for it. "We were only boys of eighteen after all," Romer said, "and badly outnumbered." The Germans leaped to the side of the road. Romer fired his Verey light into the air "and then they ran like hell. They were joined by a comrade, a Pole, who like them was fleeing for his life."

They ran for 100 meters, then hid in some thick bushes. "Firing had started all round the bridge behind them before they reached the bushes and they could see tracer bullets whizzing in all directions. It was clear that the enemy were rooting out the rest of the German garrison. Romer and his two comrades pushed back further into the bushes, very frightened, glad it was dark."

They stayed through the day and saw the whole battle—Sergeant Thornton blowing up the tank, the arrival of the Commandos, everything. They stayed through the night and well into the next day. Finally hunger and thirst forced them to surrender. "They hesitantly approached the bridge with their hands up and they were very surprised and thankful when the British did not fire on them. They knew that it was the end of the war for them and they were not sorry. They were taken to England as POWs and later to Canada where Romer said it was 'heaven on earth.'"

Howard's account concludes: "Romer and Erwin showed Howard exactly where they stood as sentries in June 1944, pointing out RAF fighter bullet marks on the steel girders of the bridge, the result of a straffing they had [received] only a few days before D-Day. They then slowly retraced their steps up the road and showed Howard where they [lay] hidden in the bushes for over thirty-six hours on that terrifying occasion forty-two years before."

In interviews with the glider pilots, Howard has provided another badly needed corrective to the first edition of this book. At the fortieth anniversary, the three pilots who landed at the canal bridge were reunited for the first time since D-Day. Together, they made a discovery, as described by Howard: "It soon became clear from the exchange of views between Boland (pilot of #2) and Barkway (of #3), plus what Howard had gleaned over the years from surviving passengers in the two gliders, that just before landing, Boland had seen Barkway's glider bearing down on him from behind, causing Boland to swerve right, while Barkway seeing Boland's glider in front of him had to swerve left and then right, turning ninety degrees and finishing up with the glider broke in half and his cockpit in the pond."

Armed with this testimony and evidence, Howard had the bronze plaques marking where the No. 2 and 3 gliders landed, switched around. This is a good example of why history is never definitive—there is always something new to be learned.

* * *

In the decade since the fortieth anniversary, the following men have passed on:

Glider Pilot Boland
Colonel Taylor
Sergeant Ollis
Corporal Godbolt
Corporal Porter
Corporal Stacey
Private Jackson
Private O'Donnell
Private Bleach
General Sir Nigel Poett
Sergeant Major Bailey
Major Fox
Major Smith

The men of Pegasus Bridge who can still answer the roll call are living happy lives, sweetened because people frequently recognize them as heroes, a role they earned and carry out with appropriate modesty.

Wally Parr's Irene died, and he has remarried, a French widow who can't speak English. Wally can't speak French. They live in Normandy and are delighted with each other and themselves.

Jim Wallwork is fully retired. He spends his winters in Mexico. He returned to England in 1992 for a reunion of the Glider Pilot Regiment and a visit with John Howard. The number of men attending the ceremonies on June 5–6 goes up each year, as do the crowds.

John Howard is a widower now. He lives in an apartment in a renovated old country mansion down in Surrey.

He has aches and pains but he soldiers on, living an exceptionally busy life. He crosses to the Continent three or four times a year, driving his own car, to lecture young cadets from the various NATO countries and Sweden—and of course for the anniversary ceremonies in June. He flies to the United States once a year, to give lectures and see friends. He keeps up a vast correspondence.

With General Poett and Colonel Taylor gone, Major Howard is the senior surviving member of the 6th Airborne Division mentioned in this book, a role he fills with distinction. His vigorous leadership has been critical to saving the bridge and the Gondrée Café. Thus he enjoys the satisfaction of knowing that just as he was the individual most responsible for the capture of the bridge, intact, in 1944, so is he the individual most responsible for the preservation of the bridge, intact, in 1994.

EPILOGUE

THE SIGNIFICANCE OF PEGASUS BRIDGE

WHAT DID IT all mean? Because the operation was a success, we can never know its full significance; only if it had failed would we know the real value of Pegasus Bridge. As it is, any assessment of the operation's worth is speculative. But then speculation is the secret vice of every history buff, and in any case is unavoidable when passing judgments.

Suppose, then, that Major Schmidt had managed to blow the bridges. In that event, even if Howard's men held both sides of both waterways, the easy movement back and forth that the British enjoyed over the bridges through the night would have been impossible. Howard could not have brought Fox's platoon over from the river to Bénouville, and Thornton would not have been at the T-junction with his Piat. The most likely outcome, in that case, would have been a failure to hold the ground in the Bénouville-Le Port area, with the result being the isolation of the 6th Airborne east of the Orne.

Had Thornton missed with his Piat, and German tanks had come down to the bridge from Bénouville, the enemy surely would have expelled the invaders. In that case, with the bridges in German hands, the 6th Airborne would have been isolated, in a position comparable to that of the 1st Airborne later in the war in Arnhem, unable to receive supplies or reinforcements, immobile, lightly armed, trying to fight off German armor. But for the bridges, in other words, the 6th Airborne might well have suffered the devastating losses the 1st Airborne did suffer.

The loss of a single division, even a full-strength, elite division like the 6th Airborne, could by itself hardly have been decisive in a battle that raged over a sixty-mile front and involved hundreds of thousands of men. But 6th Airborne's mission, like the division itself, was special. Eisenhower and Montgomery counted on General Gale to hold back the Germans on the left, making Gale the man most responsible for preventing the ultimate catastrophe of panzer formations loose on the beaches, rolling them up, first Sword, then Juno, then Gold, then onto Omaha. Gale was able to hold off the German armor, thanks in critical part to the possession of Pegasus Bridge.

Denying the use of the bridges to the Germans was important in shaping the ensuing campaign. As Hitler began bringing armored divisions from the Pas de Calais to Normandy, he found it impossible to launch a single, well-coordinated blow. There were two major reasons. First, Allied air harassment and the activities of the French Resistance slowed the movement to the battlefield. Second, the only area available to the Germans to form up for such a blow was the area between the Dives and the Orne. The natural line of attack would then have been over Pegasus Bridge, down to Ouistreham, then straight west along the beaches. That area had the further advantage of being closest to the Pas de Calais. But because the 6th Airborne held its bridgehead and controlled Pegasus Bridge, such divisions as the 2d Panzer, the 1st SS Panzer, and the famous Panzer Lehr were forced to go around bombed-out Caen, then enter the battle to the west of that city. As a consequence, they went into battle piecemeal and against the front, not the flank, of the main British forces. In the seven-week-long battle that followed, the Germans attacked again and again, using up the best and much of the bulk of their armored units in the process. Throughout this campaign, 6th Airborne held its position, thereby continuing to force the Germans into costly and ineffectual direct attacks.

What did it all mean? At a minimum, then, failure at Pegasus Bridge would have made D-Day much more costly to the Allies, and especially to the 6th Airborne Division. At a maximum, failure at Pegasus Bridge might have meant failure for the invasion as a whole, with consequences for world history too staggering to contemplate.

APPENDIX

POETT'S ORDERS TO HOWARD

5 Para Bde 00 No. 1 Appx. A

Ref Maps. 1/50,000 Sheets 7/F1, 7/F2 TOP SECRET
1/25,000 Sheet No. 40/16 NW *2 May 44*

To: Maj R. J. Howard, 2 Oxf Bucks

INFM

1. **Enemy**
   (a) Static def in area of ops.
   Garrison of the two brs at BENOUVILLE 098748 and RANVILLE 104746 consists of about 50 men, armed with four LAA guns, probably 20 mm, four to six LMG, one AA MG and possibly two A Tk guns of less than 50 cm cal. A concrete shelter is under constr, and the br will have been prepared for demolition. See ph enlargement A21.
   (b) Mobile res in area of ops.
   One bn of 736 GR is in the area LEBISEY 0471—BIEVILLE 0674 with probably 8 to 12

tks under comd. This bn is either wholly or partially carried in MT and will have at least one coy standing by as an anti-airtpo picket.

Bn HQ of the RIGHT coastal bn of 736 GR is in the area 065772. At least one pl will be available in this area as a fighting patrol, ready to move out at once to seek infm.

(c) State of Alertness.

The large scale preparations necessary for the invasion of the Continent, the suitability of moon and tide will combine to produce a high state of alertness in the GERMAN def. The br grn may be standing to, and charges will have been laid in the demolition chambers.

(d) Detailed infm on enemy def and res is available on demand from Div Int Summaries, air phs and models.

2. Own Tps

(a) 5 Para Bde drops immediately NE of RANVILLE at H minus 4 hrs 30 mins, and moves forthwith to take up a def posn round the two brs.

(b) 3 Para Bde drops at H minus 4 hrs 30 mins and is denying to the enemy the high wooded ground SOUTH of LE MESNIL 1472.

(c) 6 Airldg Bde is ldg NE of RANVILLE and WEST of BENOUVILLE at about H plus 12 hrs, and moves thence to a def posn in the area STE HONORINE LA CHARDONNERETTE 0971—ESCOVILLE 1271.

(d) 3 Br Div is ldg WEST of OUISTREHAM 1079 at H hr with objective CAEN.

3. Ground

See available maps, air ph and models.

INTENTION

4. Your task is to seize *intact* the brs over R ORNE and canal at BENOUVILLE 098748 and RANVILLE 104746, and to hold them until relief by 7 Para Bn. If the brs are blown, you will est personnel ferries over both water obstacles as soon as possible.

METHOD

5. Composition of force

(a) Comd Maj RJ HOWARD 2 OXF BUCKS

(b) Tps D Coy 2 OXF BUCKS less sp Brens and 3"M dets.
two pls B Coy 2 OXF BUCKS
det of 20 Sprs 249 Fd Coy (Airborne)
det 1 Wing Glider P Regt

6. Flight plan

(a) HORSA gliders available 6.

(b) LZ X. triangular fd 099745. 3 gliders.
LZ Y. rectangular fd 104747. 3 gliders.

(c) Timing. First ldg H minus 5 hrs.

7. Gen Outline

(a) The capture of the brs will be a coup de main op depending largely on surprise, speed and dash for success.

(b) Provided the bulk of your force lands safely, you should have little difficulty in overcoming the known opposition on the brs.

(c) Your difficulties will arise in holding off an enemy counterattack on the brs, until you are relieved.

8. Possible enemy counter-attack

(a) You must expect a counter-attack any time after H minus 4.

(b) This attack may take the form of a Battle gp consisting of one coy inf in lorries, up to 8 tks and one or two guns mounted on lorries, or it may be a lorried inf coy alone, or inf on foot.

(c) The most likely line of approach for this force is down one of the rds leading from the WEST or SW, but a cross-country route cannot be ignored.

9. Org of def posn

It is vital that the crossing places be held, and to do this you will secure a close brhead on the WEST bank, in addition to guarding the brs. The immediate def of the brs and of the WEST bank of the canal must be held at all costs.

10. Patrolling

(a) You will harass and delay the deployment of the enemy counter-attack forces of 736 GR by offensive patrols covering all rd approaches from the WEST. Patrols will remain mobile and offensive.

(b) Up to one third of your effective force may be used in this role. The remaining two thirds will be used for static def and immediate counter-attack.

Emp of RE

11. (a) You will give to your Sprs the following tasks only, in order of priority:-
Neutralising the demolition mechanisms.
Removing charges from demolition chambers.
Establishing personnel ferries.

(b) In your detailed planning of the op you will consult the CRE or RE comd nominated by him in the carrying out of these tasks by the RE personnel under your comd.

12. Relief

I estimate that your relief will NOT be completed until H minus 3 hrs, ie, two hrs after your first ldg. One coy 7 Para Bn will, however, be despatched to your assistance with the utmost possible speed after the ldg of the Bn. They should reach your posn by H minus 3 hrs 30 mins, and will come under your comd until arrival of OC 7 Para Bn as in para 13(b).

INTERCOMN

13. (a) You will arrange for an offr or senior NCO to meet CO of 7 Para Bn near their Bn RV at H minus 4 hrs 30 mins with the following infn:-

(i) are brs securely held?
(ii) are brs intact?
(iii) are you in contact with enemy, and if so where, and in what strength?
(iv) if brs are blown, state of ferries?
(v) where is your coy HQ?

In addition you will give a pre-arranged sig from the

brs, to show that they are in your possession, about H minus 4 hrs 15 mins.

(b) OC 7 Para Bn will take over comd of the brhead and of your force on his arrival at the EAST br.

MISC

14. Glider Loads

(a) Outline

Gliders 1–4. One rifle pl less handcart
5 Sprs.

Gliders 5–6. One rifle pl less handcart.
5 men Coy HQ.

(b) Detailed Load Tables will be worked out by you in conjunc with the RE and Bde Loading Offr.

15. Trg

The trg of your force will be regarded as a first priority matter. Demands for special stores and trg facilities will be sent in through your Bn HQ to HQ 6 Airldg Bde. Until further notice all orders and instrs to you on trg will either originate from or pass through HQ 6 Airldg Bde.

Both Bde HQ will give you every possible help.

NIGEL POETT
Brig.
Comd 5 Para Bde

APO ENGLAND.

ACKNOWLEDGMENTS

I WISH I could think of an adequate way to express my thanks to every person I interviewed, for the hospitality and helpfulness. Without exception, I was welcomed into homes, always offered a meal and/or a drink, frequently invited to spend the night. In the process of doing two dozen interviews in England, I got to see a great deal of the country, which was fun, and to see a great deal of the British people, which was fascinating. I stayed with old-age pensioners, with successful businessmen, with solicitors, on grand country estates, in East End flats, in fashionable West End town houses. D Company, I came to realize, came from every part of British society, with each part making its own contribution to the organization as a whole.

Their friendliness toward me, an unknown Yank prying into their past, I shall never forget. It has been a great privilege and pleasure to have had the opportunity to meet these men and women and to listen to their stories.

Adam Sisman, my editor, provided enthusiasm, energy, and exceptional efficiency, all of which was gratefully and profitably received.

I would also like to thank the University of New Orleans and the Board of Supervisors of the LSU System. In the fall of 1983 the Board granted me a sabbatical leave, which made it possible for my wife and me to live in London and travel on the Continent, and in Canada, doing the interviews. Without that sabbatical, there would be no book. My gratitude to the University of New Orleans and the Board is deep and permanent.

My wife, Moira Buckley Ambrose, carried her share of the load with her usual aplomb. As always, she worked hard with me and for me; as always, without her it would not have happened.

SOURCES

THE INFORMANTS (LISTED in the order the interviews were done): Jim Wallwork, John Howard, Wally Parr, Dennis Fox, Richard Todd, Nigel Poett, Nigel Taylor, M. Thornton, Oliver Boland, C. Hooper, E. Tappenden, Henry Hickman and Billy Gray (a joint interview), David Wood, John Vaughan, R. Ambrose, Jack Bailey, Joy Howard, Irene Parr, R. Smith, H. Sweeney, E. O'Donnell, Thérèsa Gondrée, and Hans von Luck.

My information on Private Helmut Romer comes from a note Romer sent John Howard, from a POW cage, in late 1945, after reading about Howard and the coup de main in a newspaper. Private Vern Bonck's story I got from Wally Parr. Major Schmidt's story came from various British, German, and French sources. Georges Gondrée left a written account of his activities. Lieutenant Werner Kortenhaus kindly wrote me an eight-page letter on his experiences; I want to thank Scotty Hirst for putting me in touch with Kortenhaus.

John Howard very kindly lent me all his notes, diaries, photographs, orders, and intelligence reports. Jim Wallwork gave me a copy of his written report on operation Deadstick.

I read all the standard books. The ones I found most helpful were Napier Crookenden, *Drop Zone Normandy*; General Richard Gale's *Call to Arms* and *The 6th Airborne Division in Normandy*; the official account of the British airborne divisions, entitled *By Air to Battle*; Sir Huw Wheldon, *Red Berets into Normandy*; Milton Dank, *The Glider Gang*; Hillary Saunders, *The Red Beret*; Barry Gregory, *British Airborne Troops*; James Mrazek, *Fighting Gliders of World War II*; David Howarth, *Dawn of D-Day*; Cornelius Ryan, *The Longest Day*; and Michael Hickey, *Out of the Sky*.

INDEX

In 1992, the U.S. Congress authorized the building of the National D-Day Museum in New Orleans, on the site where the Higgins Boats were constructed and tested. The Museum's mission is to remind the American people of the day when the fury of an aroused democracy was hurled against Nazi-occupied Europe, and to inspire future generations by showing that there is nothing this Republic cannot do when everyone gets on the team.

In addition to hands-on displays, a photographic gallery, weapons, uniforms, and other artifacts, the Museum will house an Archives that will hold all printed work on D-Day, plus the oral and written memoirs from participants in the battle that the Eisenhower Center at the University of New Orleans has been gathering since 1983. This is the largest collection of eyewitness accounts of a single battle in the world.

For information on how to become a Friend of the Museum, or to donate artifacts, please write the Eisenhower Center, University of New Orleans, New Orleans, LA, 70148.